MUF*CKA

MUF*CKA

A BOLD NEW PERSPECTIVE ON

GROWTH, HEALING, AND SELF ACCEPTANCE

REGGIE HATHORN

Copyright © 2021 by Reggie Hathorn LLC

MUFUCKA: A Bold New Perspective on Growth, Healing and Self-Acceptance

ALL RIGHTS RESERVED. No part of this publication may be reproduced, stored, in a retrieval system, or transmitted in any form or by any means, electronic, mechanical, photocopying, recording or otherwise without the prior permission of the publisher or in accordance with the provisions of the Copyright, Designs, and Patents Act 1988 or under the terms of any license permitting limited copying issued by the Copyright Licensing Agency. The views expressed in this work are solely those of the author and do not necessarily reflect the views of the publisher, the publisher hereby disclaims any responsibility for them.

Cover Design: Reggie Hathorn LLC
Photo Credit: Reggie Hathorn
Back Cover Design: Reggie Hathorn
Photo Cover: Yolanda Jones
Content Editor: LaShonda Watson

ISBN:

979-8-9850773-0-8 (Hard Cover)
979-8-9850773-1-5 (Paper Back)
979-8-9850773-2-2 (eBook)

Printed In The United States

AUTHOR'S NOTE

I changed a name or few in this book for whatever reason. A date or two may be off, but all the shit that's in this book is true.

INTRO

I've been trying to write a book about my life for years, probably since the '90s. Every few years I have some major revelation or I accomplish some shit and I say to myself, *Reggie it's time to write a book about your life.* I would always come up with the title before I wrote one damn word. Then I'd start writing, finish at least one chapter and then toss that shit in the trash or delete the file. I've gone through tons of titles - *The Hand You Were Dealt, Changing the Game, I Am Phoenix, Up From The Ashes, Scarred, Two-Faced, I Can Laugh Now* - those are just the ones I remember. None of them mufuckas made it.

The last time I tried to write one was spring of 2018, and that one was *I Can Laugh Now*. Honestly, I have no idea what that book was going to be about. I just liked the title. One day I laughed at some shit somebody said about me that years ago had made me cry. I said, "Aww shit! That's the title of my book. I'm bout to start writing." I wrote one chapter, shared it with a few people, and then deleted the damn file. That's just how I did shit.

At the end of 2018, I sat next to a dude on the plane that I recognized from a few Netflix specials and a lot of Spike Lee movies when I was flying back to Los Angeles from Atlanta. We hit it off, and he kinda became my mentor. I felt like he was qualified because of his experience in acting, film, and he had a cool uncle vibe. And not only that, I admired his work. He always gave me sound advice and pointed me in the right direction. He told me when I was ready to tell my story he'd help.

In Jan of 2020, I took him up on his word. I hit him up and told him I was ready to tell my story.

He asked, "Which story are you ready to tell?".

Confused, I asked, "What the hell you mean which story?"

He said, "We all have more than one story. We have tons of stories. Which of your stories are you ready to tell?"

I couldn't even say shit.

He said, "Well, write one page describing your story, email it to me and we'll go from there."

I hung that phone up mad as hell. How this mufucka gone ask me which story - hell, *my* story. I ain't bout to write one page on shit. I ain't gone send this dude a got damn thang. Fuck him.

A couple months later the pandemic struck the world, and life as I knew it had changed. Hell, it changed for everyone, and it affected us all in different ways. It was a catalyst of change for me. I picked up and moved to Chicago from Los Angeles in the thick of it. You know how it is when you move - you get a chance to discover and experience new shit and a chance to start over. That's exactly what I did, I started over and experienced new shit.

I was in a new environment, breathing different air, seeing new shit. I started taking these morning walks that would last for hours. I was walking down paths I'd never walked and taking turns I had never taken - the shit was lovely.

I spent more time by myself than I ever had. I journaled more than I'd ever journaled in my life. I was more self-reflective than ever - shit, I had time to be. It was a pandemic. I took some deep dives into my past. I revisited some really dark moments - moments that broke my ass. I realized how much I had healed and gotten past those broken moments. I was becoming okay with all of it. In spite of all the changes that were going on with the world, I was beginning to accept things as they were - including myself. I thought, *Damn, am I changing? Is a mufucka over here growing and healing? Is a mufucka learning how to accept shit for what it is?*

The answer to all of them was **yes**.

It hit me, *Ahhh now I get it. Now I see what he meant by "which story do you wanna tell".* Well, ain't that some shit. As usual, he pointed me in the right direction.

So, I decided to tell my story of growing through the brokenness, how therapy played a huge part in my healing and how I got to the point of accepting and loving myself for who I am.

So, that's the story you're bout to read - and it's called *Mufucka*.

Enjoy.

See you at the end

TABLE OF CONTENTS

Author's Note	II
Intro	I
CHAPTER 1: I CAN ONLY BE ME	1
CHAPTER 2: THE YARD	13
CHAPTER 3: SHIT HAPPENS	25
CHAPTER 4: FAMILY VACATION	35
CHAPTER 5: TKO IN THE THIRD	43
CHAPTER 6: A FIGHT IN THE STREETS	51
CHAPTER 7: THE WEDDING SINGER	59
THE AFTERTHOUGHT: WHAT DA FUCK THEY SAYING?	67
CHAPTER 8: CIRCLING BACK	71
CHAPTER 9: I AM NOT OKAY	77
CHAPTER 10: FIRST DAY OF THERAPY	87
CHAPTER 11: ANOTHER THERAPY SESSION	97
CHAPTER 12: I'M MAD	107
CHAPTER 13: LOOKING FOR A FIGHT	117
THE AFTERTHOUGHT: CHOKE THAT LIL NIGGA	125
CHAPTER 14: SMILING IN AND OUT	127
CHAPTER 15: YOU GOT IT FROM HERE	133

CHAPTER 16: AHA MOMENT	139
CHAPTER 17: YOU'RE NOT FUNNY	151
CHAPTER 18: A THOUSAND WORDS	161
CHAPTER 19: CROSSING THE BRIDGE	169
A Word For My Parents	191
A Message To The Readers	193
Acknowledgement	197
About The Author	199

CHAPTER 1
I CAN ONLY BE ME

I remember sitting in the Flick Movie Theater in 1988 getting ready to watch Spike Lee's "School Daze". The Flick was a small two-screen movie theater right behind our neighborhood, Jefferson Heights. Me and the kids I grew up with called it the Heights. There was a trail that led to the Flick through my backyard. So, from time to time, you would see random kids walking through our backyard to get to the movie theater, the arcade and other stores.

    I was there with some of my homies from the Heights. They were five of my closest friends. We all had totally different personalities. One was real chill and athletic, Stins. Another was kinda loud, nerdy, cool and really into sci-fi, MD. Another was really loud, funny and talked really fast, Lert. The oldest one was really into music, was very protective, and could fight his ass off, B. Romel. And then we had one girl with us, Alisa. She was a tomboy, played football with us and could play the hell outta some Spades. And then there was this chubby, smart, outgoing kid, Hathorn - that's me. We were the perfect crew.

Anyway, we were at the movies and Alisa was known for sneaking in home cooked food. So, our whole row smelled like hot buttered popcorn, Now and Laters, Whoppers and the home cooked food Alisa snuck into the theater. All you heard was shit talking, laughter and foil unwrapping from the fried chicken, mac-n-cheese, fried bologna sandwiches with the burnt edges. Her mama always gave her good shit. We would be laughing at her ass, but that didn't stop us from begging.

We were all excited about seeing this movie about going to a Black college since we were all just a few years from going to college ourselves. And plus, all the other movies were about white kids going to school. White kids lives. Shit, this movie was about us. Hell, we grew up in a town with a Black college. We grew up going to homecoming parades, watching black bands perform. We knew about going to football games and watching the fraternities and sororities wear their letters and step. So, we knew about what we saw on the surface, but watching the movie would let us see what happens on a deeper level. We were ready to see what the Black college experience was really like. B Romel was already in college at an HBCU, so I was thinking this movie would hit him a little different because he was already experiencing some of this shit.

As we watched the movie, I remembered how my friends laughed at damn near every scene. But my ass was over there like, *Damn this movie is more than just stepping and watching the bands marching.* It was showing these different groups of Black college students who all appeared different but who were all going through the same shit. They were talking about colorism, which is still a thing and how some people thought they had it easier than the next. Well, imagine that shit. But, I was fake laughing my ass off with my friends. I mean, I was leaning back, slapping my knee and everything. I was even saying "Big Brother Dean Almightee" like the shit was cool and hilarious. My friends were eating that shit up. But what we were doing was some corny shit because the movie was much more than that to me.

Let's not even talk about how they all went crazy on the homecoming scene when they played "Da Butt". Hell, the entire theater went crazy. Folks were getting up dancing in the aisles and shit. Not me tho. I was sitting there like, *These mufuckas just happy to be out the house at night time. This shit is not that good.* I just sat there and watched them have a good time. I mean the girls were fine, and there was ass all over the screen, but the shit didn't move me.

I don't like the song, and to this day, I hate when the shit comes on because you see all these mufuckas over 40 get up and try to relive their glory days. Not me tho. I'm the dude in the corner looking at everybody thinking, *You really don't like that song.* It was just some popular shit when you were coming up, and you want a reason to bounce yo ass. *Sit yo punk ass down.* But anyway.

Aside from "Da Butt", I did like most of the homecoming scene, including the part with Phyliss Hyman because I thought her voice was amazing, and she was so damn pretty. Her death still fucks me up. But the part that got me the most was this young black dude, Keith John. That shit was so profound that I remember the whole mufuckin' scene. I even remember what dude was wearing. He had on a kente cloth beanie, a black suit, and a blue and white stole. All he did was sit on the steps on the stage in front of the mic and sing a song called "I Can Only Be Me". That's some shit I will never forget.

When he sang, the whole theater was quiet. I did overhear a couple folks talking about how boring the song was, but my ass was quiet as hell trying to remember every word. I wish I could include the lyrics to the shit, but you know how copyright shit is, and I'll be damned if I give a mufucka any of my money from this book. But when he sang about wishing you were someone other than yourself, my ass was thinking, *I'm always wishing I was someone else.* I can't begin to tell you how many times I had wished that. I had always felt my friends were happier than me because they didn't have the problems that I had. Hell yeah, I wished I was them. Why wouldn't I? I thought they had it easier than me.

So much came over me as I listened to the song. It made me think about my boys that my female friends asked me about, "Jason is cute. Can you hook me up?" Those dudes. I never had one of my boys come to me and say, "Stacy likes you, and she wants to hook up." I just used the names Stacy and Jason as examples. I didn't know a mufucka named Jason. But I always wanted just one mufucka to come to me and say that some girl liked me and wanted to hook up. But I wanted it to be a girl I liked. So, hell yeah, I wished I was another mufucka - someone other than who I was. Why wouldn't I?

I cried on the inside when I heard those damn words. As I listened, I was thinking, *Who is this mufucka? Does he know me?* That was my shit. That's the shit I was talking about. That was the shit I was going thru. You ever heard a song that just hit you in that spot, like they wrote that mufucka just for you? That song was doing that for me.

The song is about loving yourself and being who you are. Those words hit me in a special place because I had finally heard a song that described my life. And plus, the mufucka sounded like Stevie Wonder. And you can't go wrong sounding like Stevie's ass. I mean, c'mon.

That song alone made me appreciate the movie. I still didn't like it as a whole. But I did appreciate that scene.

On the walk home through the trail, everybody was reciting all the lines that would someday become classic movie lines, and talking about how fine the girls were in the movie, where they wanted to go to college, what fraternity they wanted to pledge. I think all of us said we wanted to pledge Que Dog. We even started stepping on the trail. We all looked to B. Romel to see how he was doing it and copied him. I'm sure he was closer to doing it right than we were because was already a freshman at an HBCU. He probably saw that shit everyday. We had no idea what we were doing, but all knew how to bark like a Que Dog. I'm sure we woke up some of the white folks in the trailer park that led to our neighborhood. But we didn't give a fuck. Mufuckas walking thru the woods talking bout "WAAKE UUPP!" Hell, we had no idea what that even meant in the movie. We probably woke up some white folks in the trailer park yelling that shit, but we didn't give a fuck.

Eventually, I slid to the back of the group, so I could hum my new song and sing it low to myself. I was not about to forget the words or the tune to that shit. This is because I had this burning desire to love myself and to truly be myself. I also wanted others to be themselves as well. I always felt like that would be liberating because not loving or being yourself definitely felt like bondage to me.

When the "School Daze" soundtrack dropped, I bought it, and the only song I played for at least a month was "I Can Only Be Me." I wrote the words down and committed them to memory. It had become one of my theme songs. I promised myself that when I made it big, it would be the song I walked out to when I performed. But what was I going to do? Hell, I wasn't going to sing. I couldn't play an instrument. So, I had no fucking idea. But I felt like I would be on stage someday. I had been playing dress up by myself since I was a lil dude. I would put on a suit, walk around my room and practice introducing myself.

"Ladies and gentlemen, coming to the stage - REEGGIEEEE HAAATHOOORRN."

The crowd would go wild. I would bow 'n shit, point at a couple of folks in the audience. I saw Sammy Davis, Jr. and Frank Sinatra do that.

"Thank You! Thank You! Stop. Stop. You guys are too much. Cut it out. Aw c'mon. You're killin' me."

I was corny as shit, hahaha! All the kids I knew were trying to form rap groups and dance, but my ass wanted to come out on stage like Frank Sinatra and Sammy Davis, Jr. Hell, I still do, hahaha. I did rap for a while though. I was a natural, to be honest. I called myself "The Educated Rapper". Ya boy had bars. I would be the guy in the center of the circle spittin' lyrics at the bus stop or outside during lunch with mufuckas beat boxin'. I would hit yo ass with tha, "This is a story bout the kids in the Heights and kids rushed home when they saw the streetlights." BOOM Mufuckas! Haha. That shit would get us hype as fuck. And all my friends would be saying, "DAAAAANG! Man, that was sweet. Man, that was fresh." But I would have rather them mufuckas had been saying,

"Ladies and gentlemen, coming to the stage - REEGGIEEEE HAAATHOOORRN."

But anyway. I'm bout to get carried away, hahaha. None of that rapping shit was really me. I did it because I was kinda good at it, I liked poetry, and it was popular to be a rapper. And who didn't want to be popular at that age? Well, I know some mufuckas who didn't, but you get what I'm saying.

In real life, my ass is really like Carlton Banks because we have the same taste in music. I don't dance like that mufucka tho. I would like to think I'm a little smoother than that. People who really know me know I'm a cool ass Carlton. That's the real Reggie. I will Neil Diamond, Barry Manilow, Sammy Davis, Jr yo ass to death.

I kinda think I was always in touch with who I was. Hell, I think we all are. But having the courage to be that person is the hard part. Where do you get that courage? How do you get to the point where you just don't give a fuck and just be you? That was my struggle. Why the fuck was I thinking about this at sixteen tho? Was that normal? Shit, I don't know. That wasn't a conversation I was trying to have with my other 16-year-old friends tho.

Can you imagine you and ya boy tryna figure out what y'all gone wear to the mall to talk to some girls and yo ass break out with, "Hey man, do you have the courage to be yourself? Do you love the person in the mirror? Are you giving the world the real you?"

My boys woulda been like "Nigga, are you serious right now? Let's go to the Pines and talk to these skeezers. Tha fuck you talkin' bout ole corny ass nigga?" Yeah, not too sure that woulda made me the cool guy.

All I knew was there was some other guy trapped inside, and he wanted out. He wanted to introduce his real self to the world.

I didn't know who I could talk to about shit like that. So, I kept those thoughts and conversations to myself. But I knew that once I had the courage to be that guy, I wanted to share him with the world and inspire others to do the same. Because the shit seemed awesome.

I think you can tell that "I Can Only Be Me" triggered a lot of thought and emotions for me. There have been other songs that inspired me to live freely and be myself like "Free" by Prince, "Be Ever Wonderful" by Earth Wind and Fire, and of course, "My Way" by Frank Sinatra. But this song was different for some reason. It spoke of growth, evolution, and destiny. Even as a 16-year-old, Reggie was always my destination.

When teachers or other adults would ask what I wanted to be when I grew up, I never said anything like an astronaut, police officer, doctor, or lawyer. I would always say, "I just wanna be free and do what I wanna do when I get grown." But they would try to encourage me to choose a profession. So, I would just say engineer because I was good at math, and engineers know how to make radios. I was only concerned about radios because I wanted to make my announcement to the world that I was here. I wanted to get on the mufucka and go...

"Ladies and gentlemen, coming to the stage - REEGGIEEEE HAAATHOOORRN."

You wanna hear something crazy? I got a degree in math and electrical engineering. And I don't like doing either. I know, right! I went to school all that damn time to end up doing shit that, in my gut, I hated. I guess a lot of people do that. My ass even became a math teacher in Dallas for a couple years. I did like the kids and inspiring them and watching them grow, but a conversation with one of my pops' friends on one of my visits to my hometown put an end to that shit.

I remember the conversation like it was yesterday.

I remember his name too, but hell I don't know how to find this dude to get permission to use it. So I'm just gone call his "Pops' Boy - roll with me.

Pops' Boy: Hey Hathorn! How you been young man?

Me: Hey Mr. Pops' Boy!!! It's been a minute. Good to see you. I've been well. How are you?

Pops' Boy: Aww you know, just working and living my life. I heard you were in cold ass Minnesota. Are you still up there?

Me: Hahaha! Yeah it does get cold. No sir, I'm in Dallas now.

Pops' Boy: Ahhh Dallas. A lot of people from here are moving to Dallas. What are you doing in Dallas?

Me: Aww, I'm teaching high school math.

Pops' Boy: Awww ok. Following in ya daddy's footsteps.

What tha fuck! I ain't following in nobody's footsteps.

Me: Yeah, I guess I am, hahaha. It was good to see you, Pops' Boy.

Pops' Boy: You too, Lil Hathorn. Tell your mom and dad I said hey.

Me: Will do.

When I got back to Dallas, I quit that got damn job. I was trying to chart my own path and hearing the word "follow" just didn't sit too well with me. "You following in ya daddy's footsteps" bothered the shit outta me. It was something about hearing it said out loud. For me, hearing some shit out loud puts it in my face. It makes it real.

Even though I admired the shit outta my pops and thought he was that dude, I didn't want to follow in no mufucka's footsteps. Not even his. So, in my mind, Pops' Boy just called me "Coach Hathorn's son". Growing up, folks always called me that because my pops was a coach back in the day. But I wasn't trying to be Coach Hathorn's son anymore. As a twenty-five-year-old man, I needed to find a way to be Reggie.

That's when I started reading self-help books, watching motivational speakers and getting my hands on anything that could help me get the courage to be who I really am. Everything I found spoke on how to live your dream, how dreams come true and all that kinda shit. All that is fine, but that was not what I was looking for. None of it really spoke on being yourself. Where were the books on being yourself? Was that even a thing?

Most of my hunger to be and love myself was ignited with that one damn song. Thirty-three years later, the words still move me like they did the first time I heard them at the Flick Theater in 1988.

It's crazy that at the age of sixteen, I had one mission in life and that was to be myself, travel the world and inspire others to be themselves. I wanted people to feel free and do shit their way. You know, like Frank Sinatra. That's all I ever really wanted. And to one day be on stage so I could walk out to...

"Ladies and Gentlemen, coming to the stage..."

CHAPTER 2
THE YARD

I grew up in a small college town called Pine Bluff, Arkansas. Wait, let me be clear, I grew up in a small HBCU town. There's a difference. The black college experience is just different. We ain't got to get into all that because that ain't what this is about. But those that know - know. Ok, moving along.

If you've heard of The Bluff, which is what the natives call it, then you've definitely heard of the University of Arkansas at Pine Bluff, better known as UAPB. Home of the Mufuckin' Golden Lions. I guess you can tell I love that school because I had to put *Mufuckin* in front of Golden Lions. Well, you got damn right I do. I love the city, and I love the college. One thing I love about it is the Bell Tower. It's a big tall bell in the center of the campus surrounded by pretty green grass. It makes me feel like I'm standing in the middle of history and part of something great. If you ask me, the college is a huge part of the glue that holds the Bluff together. Let me add, some of the coolest mufuckas in the world came through the Bluff. It's a fact.

But anyway, folks in the Bluff call UAPB the Yard. But as much as I love UAPB, I didn't go there. I went to THEE Jackson State and when I got there as a freshman, I realized they called that shit the Yard too. So basically, that's some Black college shit. But when I refer to the Yard in this book, I'm referring to UAPB because it's the first Yard I knew. It's the Yard both of my parents graduated from, and it's the Yard I basically grew up on. Even when UAPB played Jackson State in the SWAC championship in 2012, I was cheering for MY Yard. I wouldn't have been mad if JSU had won, but I wanted MY Yard to win, and they did.

My pops played football at UAPB in the early 70s. After he graduated, he even coached there for a sec. So, I was always up there when I was a lil dude, going to practices, getting roughed up by the players, and watching films with him and the other coaches. And because of his connection with the Yard, I was able to get in a lot of games and other shit free. Everywhere I went on the Yard, people called me Coach Hathorn's son because if you saw him, you saw me.

When I was in the 5th and 6th grades, me and my boy Jabbar were the ball boys for the Golden Lions basketball team because his dad was the head basketball coach. Again, always on the Yard. It was my second home.

Oh, let me add, all this took place in the 70s and 80s because I was born in 1972. I forgot to mention that shit, my bad.

Okay, back to the Yard.

When I was growing up, UAPB hosted the NYSP, National Youth Summer Sports program during the summer. We called it Summer Sports for short. Summer Sports was the shit. You had kids between the ages of eight and sixteen from all over the city coming to it. I got a chance to meet a lot of kids from other schools. That shit was cool. I met some of my closest friends at Summer Sports. But watch this, a lot of them weren't even in the same school district as me. That shit made me feel cool when I had friends from another district. The shit made me feel like I was known all over the city because I knew a mufucka from every school. I was a city-wide nigga. I was connected.

The summer of 1981 was my first time attending Summer Sports. My pops was one of the coaches, so, again, if you saw him, you saw me. Man, riding in the car with my pops on the way there was the best. Sometimes we would stop by the drive thru at McDonalds and grab some breakfast. He'd get three sausage egg biscuits and some grape jelly. He would give one to me and keep the other two. Pops would fuck them sausage egg biscuits up. I would be over there thinkin', *Man my daddy is strong. He can eat two whole sausage egg biscuits."* Pops was a sausage egg biscuit eating mufucka.

There were a lot of sports and activities in the Summer Sports. I learned the fundamentals of basketball. I learned how to play racquetball, volleyball, badminton, and I even learned ballet. Ballet was where the girls were, so that's where I wanted to be. I even got pretty good at that shit. I could tendu my ass off. My boys would laugh, but I would be like *Fuck that. I wanna be around these little girls. Fuck you hard leg ass niggas.* Damn I haven't called a mufucka a hard leg since the 80s. Maybe hard legs was some Pine Bluff shit.

The best of all was swimming. Little Black kids in the Bluff weren't used to having access to too many swimming pools. There just weren't that many pools for us there, but the Yard was made for us. Most of us didn't know how to swim back then. Shit, I know I didn't. Hell, I almost drowned one day. I'll have to talk about that some other time. The shit is funny though. Trying to impress some little girl.

Swim days were extra special for me because I got a chance to see the girls in their swimsuits, and don't let one of my thighs touch one of their thighs while we were in the water - Lord have mercy! I would just swim around in the shallow water and thigh bump a mufucka. I would think about that thigh touch for weeks. I was mannish as hell.

The swimming pool was in the Hyper Complex. We called it the Hyper for short. The Hyper, at that time, was a state-of-the-art gym. Everything went down at the Hyper - assemblies, games, concerts - you name it. Hell, I went to my first concert there - Run DMC, Whodini, and UTFO. I was in the 9th grade. I was so close to the stage that I touched Run DMC's Adidas. Man, I could not stop staring at my damn hands and hated that I had to wash them. See what I'm talking about. I got so many good ass memories on the Yard that I get distracted.

So back to Summer Sports.

I remember after our first day of swimming, we were all extra hype on our walk to the cafeteria, which was just one block away from The Hyper. Walking down the street to the Union was a bunch of little Black kids who had just gotten out of a real swimming pool. We were still dripping with water, wearing towels around our necks. It was some cool shit when you had your towel around your neck. We had smiles on our faces. The shit was cool to see. Kids were talking about how long they could hold their breath underwater, how many flips they could do off the diving board, the deepest water they could swim in - and then you had me thinking about how many more thighs I could bump. SMH. But I still joined in on all the beautiful laughter and chatter that filled the street.

We make it to the caf, short for cafeteria on the Yard. There's even more energy and it's even louder in there because of the kids' laughter and chatter bouncing off the walls. Kids are yelling. Kids are throwing food. Kids are lined up in single file lines to get their food. It is organized chaos. Wet afros, Jheri curls, ponytails with barrettes, and straw hats are all over the place. Coaches wearing NYSP t-shirts, those short tight ass coaching shorts with socks up to their knees are yelling at kids, "I need one single file line!"; ``Hey young man!"; " Stop all that running inside."; " Young lady! Don't hit him!" It is a perfectly normal day at Summer Sports.

I'm standing in line with the C group, the younger kids between the ages of 8 and 10. We're all in line laughing and talking. I'm about the third person in line. The line moves, so now I'm at the front of it. I'm laughing so hard that I'm not paying attention, and the line is backing up. Out of the blue, a voice from the back of the line yells out.

"Hey, move up you fat burnt finger pig! You holding up the line!"

All the kids burst out laughing - all but this little girl standing behind me. I don't remember her name or how she looked. I just remember she's a girl. I'm like, *Hell, why she ain't laughing?* The laughter overpowers the noise of the cafeteria. Hell, I started chuckling too! That shit was funny.

Hell, I say to her, "Who is the fat burnt finger pig?", and she shrugs her shoulders.

Kids are still laughing. Some of them are even repeating it with laughter in their voices.

"Haha! Yeah fat burnt finger kid! Hahaha"

The little girl still doesn't laugh.

She says real gently, "I think he's talking about you."

I'm like, *He can't be talking about me.*

Then, I look around. *I'm* the first person in the line. I look down at my hand. My hand is burned. It is missing a finger. The fingers are crippled. Wait a minute! *I'm* the fat burnt finger kid holding up the line? Damn, the laughter seems to get louder as I look at my hand. They are not only laughing, but now they're pointing at me too. Is the entire cafeteria laughing at me? Are the coaches with the tight ass shorts laughing? The little girl behind me never cracks a smile.

I wonder what kid said that. I don't recognize the voice, but he sounded a little older than me. Damn, is anybody gone say who said it? Not one person is gone rat this kid out. Who said it? I've always had this image in my head of what he looked like. I even imagined him with nappy hair and a towel around his neck. I'm sure he had a towel draped around his neck because we had just finished swimming, and that was the cool thing to do.

I move slowly to catch up with the rest of the line. While I'm standing there, I look at my right hand again. I touch my face. Then, I look at my hand again. This is first time I ever really paid attention to it. My thumb is short with a rounded tip and is missing a finger nail. I'm missing a finger - an index finger. My other three fingers are crippled. They are bent and stiff, so stiff that I couldn't straighten them. This is the first time I ever recall trying to. I turn my hand over a couple times to inspect it as if I've never seen it. I touch my face again. I notice that the skin on the right side felt differently than it did on the left side.

I didn't even know it was funny until the other kids laughed. I didn't know why it looked that way. Has anyone told me I was burned? Did I forget? How did *that kid* know I was burned, and I didn't? He must have discussed it with some other folks.

I was so lost and confused. After I got my food, I went and sat at a corner table in the cafeteria by myself. Normally I would sit with my friends. But that day, I just needed to cry by myself. There was no way I was going to let anybody see me cry. I was a burnt pig, I didn't feel like I could sit with the other kids. I thought they were still laughing. I thought all the laughter in the cafeteria was about me now. That really hurt. I couldn't even eat my food. I felt so lonely as I sat and watched all the other kids laughing amongst each other, and there I was, sitting by myself. I looked around at all the other kids, and I saw that I looked different. I could see the difference. Not one other person had a scar on their face. Nobody else had a hand like mine. I didn't like being different. I wanted to be just like them. Why wasn't I like them?

What happened to me? Why did my fingers look like this? What was going on here?

My pops had lunch room duty that day. He was standing in the front of the cafeteria by the area where the lunch trays were dumped. My pops was tall, dark-skinned, and muscular. He was so tall, it seemed he could see everything that was going on in there. And, he had a pipe in his mouth, but it wasn't lit. It was just hanging out his mouth. He had on the Summer Sports coach outfit. Them tight ass coaching shorts and an NYSP t-shirt. He was in position with a whistle around his neck. If he saw yo ass running, "Hey Lil Man! Slow down. No running!"

He saw me sitting in the corner by myself. I tried to turn my head, so we wouldn't make eye contact. I couldn't look anybody in the eyes at this moment, not even him. But he caught me as I was turning my head away. He did the little 'come here' finger thing, beckoning for me. I sighed. *What does he want?* I grabbed my tray, got up slowly and headed in his direction. I mean, I was walking slow as hell. As I got closer to him, I noticed he had his left foot propped on a royal blue milk crate. Right before I got to him, he blew his whistle at some kid, and said "Hey young man, stop all that running inside. Walk".

Standing in front of him, I looked up at him while I was holding my tray.

He looked down at me and said, "Reg, why are you sitting over there by yourself? What's wrong?"

Let me tell you something - it's something about your parents asking you what's wrong that makes you just let go. The tears started rolling again. Every tear I had in my body came out of me. He took the tray out of my hand, placed it on the floor next to him, and sat down on the milk crate. He gently pulled me towards him. I stood in between his legs with tears rolling down my face. He wiped them away and asked what happened.

Me: Somebody called me a fat burnt finger pig.

He took a deep breath and looked away.

Pops: Reggie, the next time someone calls you that you say to them, 'I am burned but I'm not a pig.'

It's going to be a next time. Next time is going to really hurt me.

Me: Yes sir.

Pops: Because of this, your life is going to be a little different. People are going to pick on you because of your face and your hand. People are going to laugh at you. It's just how your life is going to be. That's just what it is for you.

Me: Yes sir.

Pops: But you can't let them see you cry. You gotta be tough. Can you be tough?

Me: Yes sir.

Pops: Do you want to come crying to me every time somebody says something about you or make you cry, or do you want to be tough?"

Me: I want to be tough.

Pops: Well good. You'll be okay. Wipe your face and gone outside and play.

I wiped my face. I reached down to pick up my tray, and he said, "I got it" as he slapped me on the butt. I put my hand in my pocket, and I ran outside to play with a smile on my face.

In that moment, in a cafeteria filled with laughter, it felt like it was just me and my pops, and I had learned some things.

I had just learned that I'm burned. I had just learned that I'm not a pig. I had learned that I'm going to be tough, I'm not going to cry, I'm going to be okay, and I'm not going to run to him whenever somebody makes me cry because I wanna to be tough.

My pops was my hero, and if he said not crying and not running to him would make me tough - what you think I'm gone do? Exactly!

Whew okay! Let me get myself together. He said the world would be cruel, and this was going to happen again. I knew I didn't want this to happen no mo. Do you think I want all them kids and coaches with tight ass shorts pointing and laughing at me again? Hell no! So, I decided to just keep my hand in my pocket because that's how all this got started in the first place. That little nappy head kid saw it and called me a burnt pig. Hmph, I am going to hide this forever. Nobody is going to see this hand again. And if someone makes fun of me and it makes me cry, I'm going to keep it to myself because I'm tough.

And I'm definitely not gone to tell my mama if someone hurts me or makes me cry because she tells my pops everything. You know how many times she said, "I'm gone tell yo daddy what you did when he gets home?" Forget that, she ain't bout to tell my pops I've been crying, and I ain't tough. I'm not gonna tell anybody when I hurt. I'm gone cry by myself until I don't cry no mo. Voila!

Yep, that's it. Problem solved. I'm bout to just shut up, not talk about my pain, cry to myself when I'm hurt, keep my hand in my pocket, and go outside and play. That was easy. My ass love playing. If that's what I gotta do to not deal with this, then there you go. I'm gone be a playing ass dude.

Who was I to argue with the strongest man I know?

And that's exactly what I did damn near all my life. It was the perfect formula for toughness.

Welp, that's the Yard for you. I guess the grass ain't always pretty on the Yard.

CHAPTER 3
SHIT HAPPENS

Let me tell you something about my boy Stanley. He has always been my boy through and through. He goes by the name Honey Bee. Well, he did when we were younger. He has two older brothers, Charles and Leslie, who about seven to ten years older than us. Charles also went by Honey Bee. He was the original "Honey Bee" tho. To this day, I'm not sure how he got the name. My pops used to be Charles' high school football coach back in the day, and, for some reason, I feel like my pops told me a honey bee was chasing him in practice or he got stung by a honey bee in practice or some shit like that, and everyone started calling him Honey Bee. I might be making that shit up. But I feel like the story went something like that. Well, Stan went by Honey Bee too. They were all some cool dudes. Great energy. In my mind, his big brothers were like my big brothers. They were all some pretty big dudes. They all had a little height on them and some deep ass voices.

I met Stan in the third grade at Edgewood Elementary, and we've been boys ever since. Stan was smart as shit, too. We also played little league football together for the Al's Liquor Eagles. We'd been looking out for each other, copying off of each other's homework and giving each test answers since the beginning. That's just how we rolled. We didn't keep score on who gave each other the homework last time. We just looked out for each other. Not only that, but we would explain the shit to each other to make sure we understood it. That's my mufucka. I didn't trust many folks to give me answers to homework, but I trusted Stan. He had proven himself over and over again, and I'd like to think I did the same for him.

In junior high and high school, we'd get on the phone damn near every night and do our math and science homework together. We were both pretty got damn good at math. We were some equation solving mufuckas. We did algebra, geometry, and trig. Can you believe we did all that shit together over the phone? So yeah, this shit went on for years. That wasn't just some one-year shit. And when we finished with our homework, we would call girls on three-way. That was the fun shit. My mama wasn't down for three-way or call waiting. She was like "If the line busy, they ass just gone have to call back." Ole mean ass, hahaha.

Stan grew up on the Westside and I grew up in Jefferson Heights. The Westside got three-way calling before we did in our area. So, Stan was the one placing all the calls. But we would both contribute to the cause. I would get girls' numbers, and he would get girls' numbers. I kept all my numbers in a little blue and red address book. I had all the honies' numbers in there. I had girls' numbers from every high school in the city in that mufucka - Pine Bluff High, Dollarway, White Hall, and Chapel. That book was precious. I guarded that shit with my life. I wish I could name some of the names I had in that mufucka. If you from The Bluff, you'd be like DAAAAMMMN! I didn't get rid of that book til my junior year of college. I coulda sold that mufuka and made a pretty little penny now that I think about it.

In the fall of 1988, one night after our call session to the ladies, Stan said some shit I'll never forget.

Stan: Hey man, my cousin Wendy saw you at the football game and she said she wanna meet you and hook-up.

NIIIGGA.

Did this mufucka just say he had a cousin that wanted to hook up with me? Did I hear this mufucka right? All my mufuckin' dreams just came true. We had just had a good study session, a good call session with at least three or four girls and now this mufucka tells me his cousin wants to meet ya boy. Mufucka, where she at? Get her on the phone right got damn now. I don't care how she look. Bring her to me.

Me: What game she see me at?

Stan: The game last week. She said you were cute and she wanna talk.

Me: How she look? Man, I don't even care. You got a picture of her?

Stan: Hahaha! She cute. Yeah man, I'll bring it to school tomorrow.

Me: Nigga, don't forget.

Stan: Man, I got you. Hahaha.

I couldn't even fucking sleep that night. Do you remember me saying how I wanted a mufucka to just call me and say, "Stacy wanna meet you and hook up?" Well here it is, but her name is Wendy.

The next day, I got off the bus on a mad manhunt for this dude. I got off my bus, went to this mufucka's bus, his locker, and the cafeteria, asking "Anybody seen Honey Bee?" I was bout to see if I could put "Anybody seen Honey Bee?" in the morning announcements. I had to see this Wendy.

I finally caught up with him, and he pulled the pic out. OMG. She was fucking gorgeous. She had brown skin, long hair. She was thick like I like 'em and had a pretty ass smile. Oh yeah, we bout to go together.

Stan told me they were gone call me on three-way that night. Can you believe this shit? Now, he was bout to be calling *me* on three-way with a pretty ass girl on the phone. Damn, the tables were turning, and I loved it.

I asked if he would let me keep the pic for a couple of periods to just look at the shit. He was my boy, so he did. I pulled that shit out and looked at it at least 50 times a period. Then I'd rub my finger across the shit and just touch her face.

I had to give it back to him by the end of the day, but I had her face etched in my memory, so I was good.

I couldn't wait to get home and finish my homework, so I could talk to Wendy and Honey Bee.

We had one house phone on the wall in the kitchen. It was beige with a long ass cord. My bedroom door opened up to the kitchen. If I opened my door, I could see the long ass cord dangling from the phone. I finished my dinner and homework, and I sat my ass right there on the foot of my bed, just watching the beige phone with the long ass cord. I waited patiently. I didn't have shit in my hand. I didn't have no music on. I didn't want to be distracted. I wanted all my energy to be on this damn call. I couldn't miss it. This some 80s shit like a mufucka, hahaha. Young mufuckas reading this book won't understand this.

I sat there and watched my mama go in and out of the kitchen. She came in a couple times and got some crackers and some Cheese Whiz. Damn, do they still make Cheese Whiz?

The third time she was like, "Why you just sitting there looking crazy?"

I was like, "Just sitting waiting on Honey Bee to call. He calling with his cousin Wendy on the phone."

She said, "I knew it had to be something dealing with a girl cuz I ain't never just saw you just sit on the edge of bed like that."

I was thinking, *Anyway, gone bout yo business, Mama.* She had no idea how important tonight was for me.

She walked back in the den.

After a few minutes, the phone rang. I got up slowly. I did a slow cool ass walk to that mufucka. I had to be cool when Wendy heard my voice. So, I yelled out but in a cool way, "Mama I got it." I was strolling to that mufucka like I had on a trench coat, a silk scarf, some Ray Bans, Stacy Adams and a fedora. I licked my lips and cleared my throat.

Me: Hello.

Caller: Hey Reggie, sweetie!

Me: *In the driest voice possible.* Hey Mrs. Denny.

Mrs. Denny: Let me talk to ya mama.

Me: Aight hold on, I'll get her.

I yelled out, "Mama telephone!!"

I loved Mrs. Denny to death, but this was one time I didn't want to hear from her ass. You get her and my mama on the phone, and that shit could last for hours. I was never going to get the call from my new girlfriend because we ain't got call waiting. Fuck!

I stood there, holding the phone, til she got to me and handed it to her.

"Mama, I'm waiting on a call. So please don't be on there all night."

She gave me such a look. I don't even have to explain the look she gave me.

She said, "Boy get yo ass out this kitchen and gone back and sit on the edge of that little bed. How you gone tell me how long I can be on the phone?"

I walked my ass back and sat on the edge of that little bed. She came and closed my door in such a pimp-like fashion. I sat there tho.

By this time, my dinner is fucking with me. My stomach is grumbling. Shit, I need to go to the bathroom. I open the bedroom door and see the phone is back on the hook. Yes, they long talking asses is off the phone. Now, I can get my call after I go the bathroom.

I am in the bathroom taking one of the best shits of my life when the phone rings again. I just know it is Wendy and Honey Bee. I get up in a dash. I run out the bathroom door. I yell out, "Mama I got." I pick up the phone.

Me: Hello.

Caller: Hey Reggie, sweetie. I forgot something. Let me speak to Louise one more time.

Me: Yes ma'am.

"Mama telephone!!"

I put the phone on the counter and walk back to the bathroom room, holding my pants up.

I'm in the bathroom finishing up when I hear my mama hang up the phone and her footsteps heading toward the bathroom. My mama has this thing where she talks to herself.

And I hear her say, "I can't believe this boy got this air on as cold as it is in here."

She says some other stuff I can't quite understand as her footsteps move closer to the bathroom.

Then, she stops, bends down, and mumbles, "What is all this brown? What is this?" as she sniffs to identify it.

Then, she says again, "*What is this brown*?" All of a sudden, I hear her voice again.

Mama: "REGINALD!!!"

Me: Ma'am!

Mama: "Did you SHIT on my floor?"

Me: Ma'am!

Mama: Nigga, you heard me! DID. YOU. SHIT. ON. MY. FLOOR?

Me: Huh!?

Mama: GET. YO ASS UP. AND GET THIS SHIT OFF MY FLOOR. THA HELL IS WRONG WITH YOU?

Me: Mama, Wendy supposed to be calling!!

Mama: I. DON'T. GIVE A. DAMN. ABOUT. WENDY! GET THIS SHIT UP NOW!!!

I wipe and walk out the bathroom. She's still standing in the hallway right next to the shit. She points at it. "I can't believe this shit. Yo grown ass shitting on the floor trying to wait on a call from some lil fast ass girl."

I just stand there for a second. I can't believe this shit either. I apologize to my mama. She says, "I hope she call after all this shit." Crazy thing, I'm really not embarrassed. I'm just like, *Well, if you had call waiting this type of shit wouldn't happen.* She turns the air off and walks back to the den.

I clean the shit up and go back and sit on the edge of my bed and watch the phone. I watch my mama go in and out of the kitchen all damn night making snacks. Why don't she just take that shit in the den with her? Shit!

Honey Bee and Wendy didn't call that night. As a matter of fact, we couldn't get Wendy on the phone for another week or two. Oh well. He later explained that her parents were real strict and she had to sneak and call me. Meh, that was too much work. Wendy and I eventually talked and met. She was hella cool and even prettier in person, but the thrill was gone.

Still I must admit, this whole situation did a lot for my confidence. I started to walk a little different after all this. My stride changed. It was like everywhere I went I had on the same leather trench coat, silk scarf, Ray-Bans, Stacy Adams, and fedora that I put on when I went to answer the phone when I thought it was Honey Bee and Wendy calling.

It wasn't that I was scared to approach girls because I wasn't. I approached girls all the time. Now, that was something I could do. A lot of dudes would be scared, but not me. Shit, that's one of the reasons my boys liked having me around because I was the one to walk up to girls, strike up a conversation and get shit started. The girls always ended up liking one of my boys and not me, but that's beside the point. Hahaha.

I just wanted a girl to think I was cute, to notice me, and to like me before I liked her. That's all I wanted - and not only *like* me first but to *say* she liked me first. I didn't want to have to turn flips, jump over ditches, or whoop a German-Shepherd's ass to get her attention either. I wanted this to happen without me having to do anything but be Reggie. I just wanted to be noticed for being myself. Simple as that. And that shit just happened. A girl noticed me at a football game while I was just chilling being myself. And the girl was cute. Can you believe that shit!? A cute girl liked me first! Nigga, I'm bout to take over the world. You can't tell me shit now. Wendy done started some shit. When a girl don't like me, I'm gone be like "Fuck you! Wendy like me. Kiss my ass!"

For the longest time, I mean years, whenever I had a low confidence moment, I would take myself back to that day Honey Bee let me hold on to Wendy's pic for those few class periods; I would pull that pic out my pocket and say "Wendy liked me" And that would get me through.

I haven't heard from or seen Wendy in over 30 years.

Welp, Wendy and I didn't end up going together like I had hoped. My mama cussed me out for shitting on the floor. I needed my ass whooped for that shit. But all this started because someone noticed me. And they noticed me while I was just being Reggie. That was the cool part.

CHAPTER 4
FAMILY VACATION

I'll be the first to admit that I didn't see a lot of happiness in my household - at least not amongst my parents. When they were with me individually, it was a good ass time.

My moms and I went shopping a lot. She was always really stylish. My moms *did* some shopping, so I was known at every lady's dressing room all over the city. People would all be amazed at how patient I was while my mom tried on clothes. I just liked seeing moms walk out the dressing room looking pretty. Besides shopping, we did all kinds of shit. We played all types of board and card games like Trouble, Candy Land, Spades, Ms. Pac Man on the Atari, and I would whoop her ass in Trivia. Yeah, I was a smart mufucka. Sometimes I'd let her win cuz she's Moms. She would deny the Trivia thing - I'm just saying.

Me and Pops would go fishing, do yard work, go record shopping at Record Rack. He would thumb thru albums, tell me stories from his heyday, and hip me to old school music. In my neighborhood, I was always the kid that had music first because of him. And I would hang with him on the Yard and be Coach Hathorn's son.

It was a lot of fun when I had them one on one. But some together shit - nah. I didn't see them laughing and having a good time together a whole lot. Not a lot of affection either. Some days I wondered if they even liked each other because I really don't recall them talking to each other much. It just wasn't a lot of happy family shit.

The only time I really remember them getting along and just kicking back and having a good time was on our family vacations - that was when they got it in. But, we weren't like other folks where we'd go to different places each time like Disney World, the Rockies, and shit like that. Our shit was always to the same places - my grandmama's(Big Mama) house for Christmas in Louisville, MS which is my birthplace and Galveston, TX.

I only say Big Mama's house was a vacation because it was at least a four to five hour drive and we were all in the car together, which was rare. You just didn't see us all in the car together. The shit is crazy now that I look back at it. I mean, I guess you can call it a holiday vacation. Big Mama's house was hella fun and she was one of my favorite people in life. So fuck it, we'll say it was a vacation.

But Galveston, now *that* was a family vacation. We were together the whole time, which was different in itself.

The ride there was everything. We always had a few vehicles. Well they did - I didn't own shit. Moms always had her car- some type of Oldsmobile or Cadillac, and my pops had an old pick up truck in the backyard. Yes, the mufucka actually ran. That was the fishing truck. He wasn't bout to just have some shit sitting in the yard that didn't work. He also had a red and black '58 Chevy that my friends called the BatMobile. Then, there was the van. It was dark blue with a lighter blue stripe going down the side. That shit was dope.

The van is what we used for the family vacations. It had a TV and a bed in the back and four seats up front. I always hung out the back because it just felt cool to be lying down while we were traveling.

My pops would always have on some kinda hat - a cowboy hat, newspaper boy hat, sailor hat, or just a simple baseball cap. That nigga loved hats. I did too tho. He would always have his pipe hanging out his mouth. A lot of the times it wouldn't even be lit. But when it was, it smelled like Captain Black tobacco or black cherry. That shit smelled good. And he would be playing all the old school jams that he and moms liked.

Moms would be in the passenger seat reading a V.C. Andrews novel, wearing her big ass sunglasses, some kinda cute hairstyle, and a summery outfit. Moms always rocked the big ass shades. Even when they went out of style for a while, she would still rock them shits. And she would be cute too. And when they came back in style, she looked like she was setting a trend, hahaha. She wore them in grocery stores, malls, boutiques- she never took 'em off. If I said "Mama, why you got yo shades on in the inside?" She would say, "I don't give a damn bout these folks. These my shades." I often think she was the first person to not give a fuck.

When we traveled, they would sing, talk, laugh, and just have a good time. I liked seeing that so I just let them have it. Every now and again, I would get between the seats and lean in and join in on the fun because it was a rarity in our household.

During every trip, we would stop by big ass truck stops along the way, and we would all get our favorite snacks. Moms would get skins (pork rinds for you Northern mufuckas), a Hostess Sno Ball, some Double Mint gum and a soda. Pops would get a honeybun, some peanuts, and some kinda soda. Me - I would get all the same shit they got and some Boston Baked Beans. Normally, they woulda tripped about me getting all that shit because I was husky, but on the family vacation, they didn't give a fuck. That was one of the best parts of the trip. Actually, it was my favorite. To this day when I travel, I always gotta stop by a big ass truck stop and get a whole bunch of shit I don't even need or want. It takes me back to those times. It's just what I do. So if you ever travel with me, just know we stopping, and I don't care if it puts us off schedule. Hahaha!

We would be snacking and laughing all the way to our final destination, Galveston, TX. Galveston is a beautiful little city on the coast of the Gulf of Mexico. It was my first time seeing any races other than Blacks and whites. That's all I saw in the Bluff. But in Galveston, I saw Latinos. At the time, I just thought they were darker skinned white folks. I had always thought that if you weren't black, you were white. And, it was my first time hearing other accents and languages in real life.

We went to Galveston because it was nice, and it was the home of Shriners Hospital for Children. The folks at the Shriners in Galveston did and still do amazing work treating burned and crippled children. I found out years later that Shriners has children's hospitals in cities across the U.S. I always said once I made it, I would go back and speak to burned children as a way to give back, to inspire them and to just be an ear for some of them because we share a similar story.

So yeah, the shit had a dual purpose. It was a family getaway - we would go to the beach, go shopping, and hang out in the hotel, but it was really for my ass to have surgeries on my head.

I was having these experimental surgeries on my scalp, so I could have a full head of hair. My hairline was pushed back because of scar tissue from my burn. When I look back at pics, I've always thought I looked like Maurice White(RIP) from Earth, Wind, and Fire. I always rocked a New Yorker - Afro Hybrid because that's all I could really do. For you mufuckas that don't know, the New Yorker is a hair style - Google that shit. Anyway, those surgeries were going to get me a full head of hair. And when they did, the first hairstyle I was going to get was a Jheri curl. Then, I was going to let that shit grow and rock a ponytail. Yeah, I was gone be fly. I just knew I was gonna be driving around with a ponytail in a red convertible playing some Prince. I just knew it. And you weren't going to be able to tell me shit.

I'm bout to close my eyes and envision that shit...hollon. Ok. I'm back.

So a full head of hair was the goal.

Going to Shriners was an eye opener. I saw kids who had lost way more than I did in the fire. I saw kids with no eyes, no arms, no ears, no legs, no noses - you name it; I saw it. It was so sad. I made me look at myself and think, *Damn, you not so fucked up after all.* I felt sorry for those kids. Shit, all I had was a missing finger, a scar on my head and face. Hmph, I bet some of those kids wished all they had was a missing finger and a scar on their face. I probably was the kid other kids in Shriners wanted to be like. I mean, I didn't like the scars on my face and missing a finger, but there were kids way worse than me. I could only imagine the shit they went through, the thoughts they had, or how they felt.

But the saddest thing to see was the kids without parents or someone there to be in the recovery room when they came out of surgery. We all shared a recovery room in an open area with about eight to ten beds. To see those kids wake up from having gone through a whole surgery with no one there to hold their hand or to just ask how they felt was heartbreaking. I can definitely say this made me appreciate my moms and pops. Because when I came out of surgery, I saw two smiling parents - my pops cracking jokes and my moms rubbing my head or my arm. This was another reason I liked the family vacations.

While in the recovery room, there were times I would wake up from a nap or whatever, and I would see my moms sitting next to these random kids' beds holding their hand, watching TV with them, reading to them or just sitting there with them. Every now and again, I'd see her tear up. She would put her big ass shades on and walk out of the room. Maybe she was hiding her tears. I don't know. Shit, they were her shades. I would also see my mom in the game room playing games with the other kids - some of the same board games she played with me at the crib. I don't think she played Spades with them tho. Though we didn't talk to each other much, I always felt like me and the other kids had a special bond. It was kinda understood. We were a team. So, I didn't mind sharing her during these moments. I guess we all need a mama in our lives. Plus, she would always mosey back over to me.

My pops would be talking to the doctors trying to get a better understanding of the procedures that some of the other kids were having. He was into the technical and procedural aspect. He later told me he had always wanted to be a surgeon because he was good with his hands and wanted to help others with his hands. He didn't do it cuz he didn't have the resources in college, so he did what he had to do. He went into education.

My procedure seemed really complex at the time. The doctors implanted a balloon - the same thing used for breast implants - underneath my scalp. They would put it in the area that had hair. So I would go to Galveston to have a balloons inserted in my head.

Once I got back to the Bluff, I would go to a doctor every week or so, and they would inject a saline solution in the balloon which would stretch my scalp. Once the balloon was at full capacity, after a couple months or so, we would go back to Galveston. The family vacation would be on repeat. Blue van, truck stops, snacks, old school music, big ass shades, hats and pipes.

The doctors in Galveston would remove the balloon, take the stretched skin, pull it over the hairless areas and staple it. Pretty neat process. I would have the staples in my head for about 10 days. My pops would remove them when it was time with a little instrument that looked kinda like a hole puncher. It got to the point I could remove them myself. In another five or six months, I'd go thru the process again. After about 5 rounds of this, I would have a complete head of hair. And I was moving through the rounds.

Awww shit…get ready Jheri curl!!! I'm coming for that ass.

So Galveston was a win-win. Family vacation and Jheri curls.

CHAPTER 5
TKO IN THE THIRD

It was the fall of '86, and I was in the middle of the third round of one of my procedures that I was having on my scalp. I was in the 9th grade. Our school ran a little different. The junior high was 7th-9th grade, so that means I was the big shit on campus. I had to have my shit together. This included getting my Jheri curl. My parents were divorced by now, but we still had the family vacation popping. Man, we had a whole system going. We would roll to Galveston, so I could get the balloons inserted. Then, I would go to the doctor in the Bluff every week or so to get the little injections to fill the balloon up. Piece of cake. Shit was working like clockwork. It was just a matter of time before I got this Jheri curl. I was actually trying to figure out if I wanted to get a S-Curl instead - decisions, decisions. I had seen a few cats with

S-Curls, and I kinda liked it. Wasn't sure yet. But I was just considering it.

The balloon that was used in my scalp was getting bigger. This meant that my scalp was being stretched. The thing about this is that it was quite obvious that something was going on with my head. I had a really big lump where the balloon was. I couldn't have everyone seeing this. It was cool tho cuz my folks worked it out with the school and my teachers so that I can wear a hat in class. So bam, nobody knows what's going on underneath the cap. It's business as usual.

So, I started getting all types of baseball caps and other styles of hats. The style changed with the size of the balloon. If the balloon was big, I rocked a newspaper boy hat and tilted the bitch to disguise it. If it was not so big, I rocked a baseball cap. It was a game to me. I had fun with it.

It felt cool to be the only kid allowed to wear hats in class and in the halls. Other dudes would get yelled at, "Young man take that hat off inside." But me, I'd just get the nod like I was in the mafia or some shit. Do they still make kids take their hats off inside? Is that still a thing?

Every now and again, some kid would ask, "Why does he get to wear a hat in class?" I remember this one teacher responding, "It's because he's so cool and smart. He gets special permission." That shit made me smile so hard. All the other kids started saying, "I'm cool and smart. Can I wear a hat?" Interesting thing tho, I won the "Best All Around Student" and the "All A's" awards in the 9th grade, so the shit seemed believable. Mufuckas knew I had the grades and shit, so it coulda been a real thing. So I rolled with it. And I was actually a cool ass nigga, so I mean, why not think it was some real shit?

We were all going into class one day, and it was rowdy as usual. Kids coming in talking shit about something that had just happened last period. Little boys pushing each other and play fighting. Some kid asking another kid for their homework. Little girls talking about what they talk about. Some kids just going straight to their seats and shutting the fuck up and getting their homework out. It was a normal fucking day at Watson Chapel Junior High. The bell rang, and a substitute teacher walked in. I really wish I remembered what the dude had on for the sake of the story. But I do remember he was a middle aged white dude with the typical white dude voice. Let's not act like we don't know what the white dude voice is.

He ordered everyone to sit down so he could take roll. He had his head down as he was reading the list and mispronouncing mufuckas' names. The usual substitute shit. And kids would break out laughing.

He got to my name and in the white man substitute voice, "Reginald Hawthorn. Do you go by Reggie?"

I kindly corrected him, "Yes. I go by Reggie. And it's Hathorn. No W."

He checked my name off and said, "I'm sorry Reggie. Got it!"

He was respectful.

He looked up and said, "Reggie if you don't mind, could you remove your hat. I don't think you're supposed to wear hats in class."

A few kids spoke up, "He gets special permission to wear hats because he's cool and gets all A's."

I sat there calmly because this was all I needed.

I was like, "Yeah you heard them."

I'm not sure if they were being funny or not. But it didn't feel like they were because I actually thought they were trying to get all A's so they could wear hats too.

But my man didn't budge. "Reggie, just follow the rules, son, and take off your hat on the inside."

"Man seriously, I get special permission. Just gone to the next person."

"Son, just take your hat off, or I'm going to send you to the office."

Fuck it. Let me take this hat off, so he can leave me the fuck alone.

I took the hat off.

A voice yelled out. "MAN!!!! DAAANNG!!! That nigga look like he got two heads. Damn nigga, what's wrong wit yo head?"

The whole class broke out in laughter. Well most of them. I sat there quietly.

He said, "I'm sorry. You can put your hat back on son."

Hell, by this time, the gig was up. It was like that day in the cafeteria on the Yard all over again. But these mufuckas were not going to see me cry because I was tough. I wanted to, but I wasn't going to let 'em see it. I wanted to ask who said it and go back there and just slap the shit out of them. Because at this point of my life, I could actually fight and wasn't fucked up about just going to slap a nigga or at least punch the nigga in the chest and knock the air out of him. But I thought about the staples and the balloon and what would happen if it burst, so I just kept my cool. That shit wouldn't be cool to be fighting and having juice, a balloon 'n shit all over my face. So I just sat there. And what was crazy was that, again, no one said who said the shit. It was some black dude. I think I knew the voice, but I was too hurt, frustrated and shocked to really investigate.

And once again, there was one little girl that didn't laugh. I remember her this time because she sat close to me. She was a little white girl named Leigh Ellen. She just kinda looked at me with sympathy in her eyes. She didn't laugh. Her eyes and energy actually comforted me and calmed me down. I never told her how her energy helped me that day, but I've always held a special place in my heart for her. Even now.

This happened in the third period, so I spent the last few periods of the day to myself. And, I did cry when I got by myself though.

People had picked on my burn and my hand throughout the years up to that day, and each time it hurt. But for some reason, this time stung like it did the first time. Maybe it was because I was hiding shit underneath my hat, and I was exposed. Or because it was said in a class full of folks. Or maybe it was because I didn't know who said it. It always hit me different when people said it to my face versus behind my back. I could take it when they said it to my face because I could see them. I knew who my so-called enemies were, but for it to be said behind my back, and actually hear the voice was different - I don't know.

I was quiet on the bus ride home. Normally, I would be joning (joning: talking shit about folks, cracking on people or playing the dozens), but that day I kept to myself and just looked out the window and watched the other kids do their normal shit.

I walked in and spoke to my mom as usual. She didn't notice anything was wrong because I was a master at keeping shit like this to myself. But on the inside, I was dying. I went into my bedroom, got on my knees at the foot of the bed and cried like it was the end of the world. I was hurt. I finished crying and changed into my after school sneakers. I went to the bathroom and wiped my face. Then, I went outside and hung with my friends like nothing had happened.

A few days later, I told my mom I didn't want to do the surgeries anymore. She asked why and I told her I just wanted to let my hair be like it was. I just wanted to stop going. Then, she asked if I was sure, and I told her yes and that I was just tired of going to Galveston.

She called and told my pops. He and I had an in person conversation about it as well. I just said, "Man I'm good. I'll be fine. I'm just tired of going down there. I'm good with my head the way it is." He asked again to make sure, I was like "Yeah Dad, I'm good."

I mean, he told me it was going to be like this. He said the world was cruel and people were going to pick on me - he predicted this shit. So what was the point of telling him someone hurt my feelings? It wouldn't do any good.

They were both like well okay, the next one is your last one then. And that was it.

No Jheri curl. No S-Curl. No ponytail while driving in the red convertible playing Prince. Just crooked hairline, space on the top of the head Reggie. But as usual, I'd be fine.

The trip to Galveston was different this time. We traveled in a car. My moms had a brown and tan '85 Nissan Maxima. We still stopped by the truck stops and got all the snacks. Pops still had his pipe, and Moms still had her big ass shades and the V.C. Andrews books. But the overall mood and energy was lower. This sealed the deal. Because my folks were divorced, I knew it was the last of the family vacations. So, if I had any hopes of them getting back together, they ended there.

When I got to Galveston and walked around Shriners, I knew it would be my last visit there as a patient. I still had an unspoken love for the other burn survivors, and in my head, we were still going to be a team. And I would always pray for them. I would always want the best for those other kids, but this was it for me.

My parents asked me one more time if I was sure. I was definitely sure.

On the way home, I just sat in the back of the car and cried to myself a little. I kept thinking, *Reggie you literally only have two to three more rounds of that procedure and you're done.* I was in the third round of those surgeries, but I just couldn't push it. No Jheri curl was worth enduring that shit again. Fuck that curl.

I went back to school like nothing had happened. No more hats in class. Back to joning mufuckas. All was well with the world.

The guy that blurted that shit out in class that day had no idea that he had delivered the knockout punch. No more family vacations. No more truck stops. No more hopes of my parents getting back together. I guess we can say it was a TKO in the Third Round.

CHAPTER 6
A FIGHT IN THE STREETS

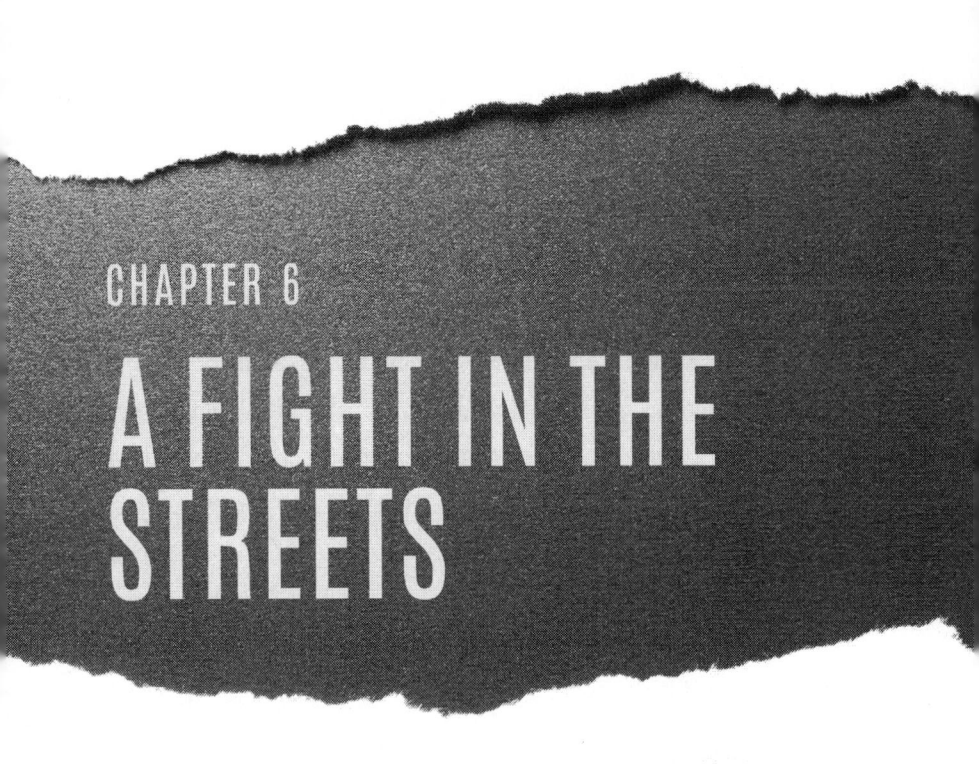

Aww shit! The summer of '87 had been fuckin' fabulous. I had spent it with my fam off of Mark Twain and 7 Mile in Detroit. Man, I love Detroit. I was kickin' ass the entire time - literally.

I spent many a day just boxing niggas in the street. Them Detroit niggas were real serious bout that shit. They had boxing gloves and shit. I was kicking niggas' asses that had reputations for being able to fight. My cousins were cheering my ass on, too. They had towels and gave me pep talks between rounds. The shit is hilarious now that I look back at it. One of my cousins was like "Damn I didn't know you could box like that!" Shit, I think more than anything, I was releasing frustration. But, them Detriot niggas were mad that some lil country nigga from the South was taxing that ass. They were like, "We need him to fight Norm." Norm was 18 years old and ripped. My ass was 14 years old and husky. But a mad 14 year old husky dude ain't no joke either. I was like, "Bring 'em on." One of my cousins was like, "Wait, cuz this nigga can fight *fight*." I was like, "So what that mean?"

I wasn't scared of shit. I could fight a mufucka I could see.

Norm and I fought for about five rounds, and they called the shit a draw. Hell, I was tired. I had just fought three or four other dudes. Norm had fresh arms and legs. Norm ended up putting his arm around my shoulder and said, "Damn lil nigga, do you box?" Norm didn't know that I had endured so much mental and emotional shit that I ignored physical blows. That was nothing. I could take a punch. I don't know if I even felt this nigga hit me. But I know he did.

I just had a TKO in the third round that past school year. But I had made up for it by knocking mufuckas out that summer. Shit always seemed to balance itself out.

Also, that summer I also got two new pairs of some fresh Adidas, and I couldn't wait to bust these out in the Bluff. It was always cool to go to the city and get some shit you couldn't get at the crib. It made me feel like a star. And, I needed that in that moment. I think Detroit may have a contract with Adidas because them Detroit niggas seem to love them. Everywhere I went, I saw Adidas. That's when I fell in love with them. And I got me some fake ass Gazelles that I ended up taking my school pic in. I was clean. You couldn't tell me shit.

I got back to the Bluff to go into my sophomore year. It was like starting over because sophomores were the babies at the high school. But the cool thing was that 11th and 12th graders were the same kidsI I had been with before in junior high. I had established some good relationships with these cats, so it was gone be cool. Plus, I got my new Adidas and some fresh new fake ass Gazelles. Shit, I was good.

Wait, did I tell y'all I was the Best All Around Student last year? I did. Aw okay, I was just making sure. Life was good.

Everybody was going back to school. Moms was a third grade teacher. So, she was starting to get her classroom together - decorating n shit. I would go over there and help move shit around, clean shit up, and hang stuff in high places that she couldn't reach.

And my pops was getting ready to go back to school too. But he was leaving the Bluff to get his PhD from Iowa State in Ames, Iowa. He was moving on from the coaching life and being a middle school principal. I guess progress is good, but that was pretty damn far. He wasn't going to be just across town anymore.

I knew he was coming by the house before he left, so I waited in my bedroom with my door closed. It was about 6:30 pm, and I was sitting on the edge of my bed thinking about all kinds of shit. I had my record player playing "Free" by Prince, which was my shit back in the day. Actually it still is. The words to that song just do it for me.

The song is about doing shit how and when you want to - about not going to bed til the sun was up, not crying unless you were happy, being free enough to change your mind when you wanted to. Sometimes you just change ya damn mind just because, and you don't wanna explain that shit. That's the type of shit Prince talks about in "Free". I love that damn song.

Look, I'm a Prince freak. So I need you to be up on your Prince when you read my shit because I just might break out a song on yo ass. If you don't know the song, go to wherever you listen to music - Spotify, Pandora, Apple Music or wherever to listen to this song before you finish this chapter. No, I'm serious. I need you to feel this shit with me.

Fans of the 1999 album are already with me. I need everybody to be together.

I'll wait.

Ok, so I was waiting on him to come by the crib to tell me and Moms bye. All kinda thoughts were running through my head: *I'm going to miss you. I want you to stay. I don't want you to leave. I **really** don't want you to leave. I need you to stay. Do you really have to leave? I need you. Don't go, you're my best friend. Please don't go.*

My moms knocked on my door. I turned down my Prince, opened it and she said, "Yo daddy's outside. I'm bout to go out here and talk to him for a sec." I just said okay, closed the door, and went back to listening to my Prince.

I heard the front door close.

Moms stayed out there for a little while. I kept getting up off the edge of the bed to put the needle back on "Free". It kept me calm. On the inside, I was dying. My best friend was leaving me. Were people going to remember I'm Coach Hathorn's son when he was gone? If I ask him to stay, am I being weak? Yeah, that's being weak. I ain't asking him shit. I'm just gone tell that nigga bye.

I heard the front door open, and my moms yelled my name. I opened my bedroom door. She was standing in the hall, almost in the exact same spot that I shat on when I was waiting on the call from Wendy. With tears in her eyes and a cracking voice, she said, "Your dad wants to talk to you." I closed my bedroom door, hugged my mom, and headed outside. The walk down the hall seemed so damn long. It wasn't a big house, but this hall seemed hella long that night. She left the big door open, so I could see his car parked outside through the screen door. He had a burgundy '86 Nissan 280 Z. It was clean, and it had T-tops. That's showing you it's old - the mufucka had T-tops. They don't even make them shits no more.

He stood outside next to the car, parked right underneath the streetlight on the corner. The light beamed down on the car like it was being showcased. The car was running, and the park lights were on. He had some music playing. I can't remember the song, but I remember the music.

I stood at the door for a sec and took a deep breath. I could still hear my mom sniffing a little in the background. I opened the door and went outside. Our house sat on a hill, so I still had a ways to go to get to him.

When I got to him, we hugged. I was straight numb. He started our conversation.

Pops: Well Reg, I'm bout to go.

Me: I know, man.

Pops: You gone be okay. I'm gone be okay. You can come visit me anytime you want to. You know that, right?

Me: Yeah, I know.

Pops: You can always call me if you need anything. You know that, right?

Me: Yep.

Pops: You know I love you, right?

Well nigga, why you leaving?

Me: Yeah, I know. I love you too.

Pops: Me and yo mom had a good talk. You gone be fine. Y'all gone be fine.

Me: Yeah, I know.

Damn, I don't want you to go.

Pops: You okay?

No nigga. I'm not okay.

Me: Yeah man. I'm good. How far you gotta go?

He went on telling me bout his drive and the route he was going to take - a bunch of shit I really didn't care to hear about. But I listened.

Pops: Okay. Well, go get ya mama.

I walk back in the house to get Moms. She was still standing in the hallway. I told her he wanted to see her, and we walked out together.

He was in the car by now. Music was still playing.

Me and moms stood next to the driver's side door and talked to him. They talked about his trip and how far the drive was and miscellaneous bullshit. Under the beam of the streetlight on our busy street, the whole damn neighborhood could see what was going on with the Hathorns. We were the show of the hour. My moms and pops - they don't seem to give a shit. They out there talkin' bout where he gone stop and rest and out I'm here having the fight of my life. *Reggie, ask him to stay. Nah, fuck that. Let him go. Nigga, don't cry. Be tough. Let me break this random bullshit up and go back in the house.*

As I was walking, I yelled back and told him to have a safe trip and to let us know when he got there, and he said that he would. When I got back to the house, I stood at the door and watched them for a sec. He got out the car and gave my mom a hug. Then, he got back in, put a pipe in his mouth, put the car in 1st, and drove off. And just like that he was gone. My dude was gone.

My moms stood there for a sec until she couldn't see his tail lights anymore. Then, she started coming back toward the crib. I rushed back to my room because I didn't want her to know I was watching their asses. I closed the door and sat back on the edge of my bed.

She tapped the door and walked in with a few tears in her eyes and said, "Well, he's gone." I said, "Yeah I know." She asked if I was okay. I told her I was. She asked if I needed anything. I told her I was good. She closed the door and went on bout her business.

I really wished he would have stayed. Damn, I wished he would have stayed. I wouldn't be able to call him if something happened. He couldn't get here in 15 minutes if something happened. He wouldn't just across town anymore. Damn, I wished he would have stayed. I really needed my daddy. But I didn't even feel comfortable telling him that. That woulda made me weak. And I had to be tough. I was going into my first year of high school tho. He picked a good ass time to leave.

I'd like to think that if I asked him to stay just til I got outta high school, he would have stayed. I wish I would have asked him to stay. I should have asked him. Too late now. He was gone. I guess I'll do what I always do - be quiet and hold this shit in. Oh well, it was nothing new.

But this bout to be a good ass year cuz I got some new Adidas and a fresh pair of fake ass Gazelles.

I sat on the edge of my bed and turned on "Sometimes It Snows in April" by Prince and cried myself to sleep.

I fought in the streets a lot that summer. I kicked ass in Detroit. I had a draw against the neighborhood tough guy who was four years older and in better physical shape than me. And I fought myself under the streetlight in my own hood, tough enough to watch my pops leave and not let him see me cry. I'd say it was a summer of kicking ass in the streets.

CHAPTER 7
THE WEDDING SINGER

Can I tell you how good I feel right now? I feel amazing. I got my Prince CD playing. The word CD already let's you know this some old shit I'm bout to talk about. It's a Tuesday afternoon in November of 2004. "Money Don't Matter Tonight" is filling up the crib. The house smells like bacon and eggs because I just smashed a bacon, egg and cheese sandwich. You already know how hard it is to get that bacon smell out your house. Just thought I'd mention that.

I'm dancing around the crib gathering all my toiletries, my favorite colognes, and my clothes. I just picked up my favorite royal blue v-neck sweater to fold it and put it in the suitcase that's sitting on the bed. When I put it in the suitcase, I patted it a couple times to make sure it was safe. I know

I'm not the only one that gives that special garment that little extra touch. I put on a little bit of cologne. I wish I could remember what fragrance it was so I could add to the story, but I don't, so use your imagination.

I'm excited because tomorrow I'm going to Atlanta to see The Wedding Singer. She was this cute little 26 year old brown skinned, pretty smiled, funny, cool ass singing girl I met at my boy Dino's wedding a couple months ago. And you got it, she was the singer. She could sing Anita Baker's "Angel" like nobody's business. "Angel" was always a special song to me because it was playing when my cousin Tammie attempted to teach me how to backwards skate at a fraternity party in college. Every time I heard the song after that, I would smile and think about how patient Tammie was as I kept fucking up my turns. Those turns would whoop my ass. When my cousin saw me wobbling, she would hold my hands and say, "It's okay cuz, you not gone fall. I got you."

So when The Wedding Singer sang this at the wedding with so much passion, it made me give her a second look and approach her. I told her how much I loved her rendition. And she told me how much she appreciated me singing "One In A Million You" by Larry Graham at the reception. She was like, "You can carry a note, but you can't sing sing, hahaha!" She had jokes. I liked that. "One In A Million You" was me and my boys' get drunk song in college. We would all hug in a circle and sing that shit to the top of our lungs. Some wild shit always happened after we sang that song. That's all I can say about that. I'm not trying to put my boys' business out in these streets.

The Wedding Singer and I had been getting to know each other since then. And we were sweet on each other. I even went back to visit a time or two. It was cool each time. Once, I went back to see her perform at some little lounge that had a cool little vibe. She was pretty good and could work the crowd. We talked on the phone damn near every night. We would just sit up and laugh and talk about everything. Every now and again, I would ask her to sing some shit, and her ass would damn near always oblige. She was one of those people that would just break out in song, kinda like me. We hadn't gotten physical or anything yet, but she hadn't seen me in my royal blue sweater either.

Please know that I'm putting this sweater in the suitcase thinking, *Yeah we either gone kiss or we gone fuck after she see me in this.* This trip, we fucking, or she at least gone ask me, "So what are we doing? Are we in a relationship or not?" cuz she is definitely gone wanna take it up a notch or two after she gets a whiff of me in this cologne that I can't remember and this sweater. You can't tell me shit when I got on Royal Blue. I think we all have that one outfit that makes us feel like we're unstoppable or like everybody is looking at us.

I'm feeling good. Now " DMSR" by Prince is playing. I'm dancing and singing hella hard. Oh, for you non-Prince fans DMSR stands for Dance, Music, Sex, Romance. Listen, if you don't know this song, please listen to it before you continue reading. We've gone over this shit before. I hope this is the last time I have to say this shit. I need you to feel me on this shit. Okay?! Thanks! The phone rings. Awww shit, it's her! Perfect timing. I already know she's calling to tell me how excited she is to see me tomorrow. Hell, I'm excited too. Let me turn this music down, so I can hear her.

I put on my Stacy Adams, my trench coat, Ray Bans, fedora and scarf - y'all know the drill. I had to get my sexy excited voice on. So I cleared my throat. Then I sat on the couch, and let the phone ring a couple of times before I answered it.

Me: Heeeyyy You! What's up?!

TWS: Hey Reggie! How are you?

Her voice was a little dry. But it's cool.

Me: I'm good. I'm excited about seeing you tomorrow.

TWS: Awww nice. So about this visit.

Me: What about it?

TWS: So you and I are getting pretty close, wouldn't you say?

Here it comes. She bout to hit me with "Sooo what are we doing?" She's ready to level up. I knew it.

Me: Yeah, I'd say so. I'm digging you.

TWS: So, I think we're at the point that this trip is a trip that I would want you to meet my friends because we're getting tight.

I knew it. I'm smiling so hard right now. She wants to go to the next level.

Me: Hm. I can see it. You've met a couple of mine, so I get it.

TWS: Yeah, but I don't want you to.

I'm so fucking confused right now. She brought the shit up just to say I don't want you to? Tha fuck is that? Mufucka, I didn't ask to meet them.

Me: I'm lost. What you mean you don't want me to? You brought it up.

TWS: Yeah I'm not ready to explain you. I'm not ready to explain your hand. Your burn. The scars on your head. I'm not ready to explain what happened to you and the stares. You know people stare at you when I'm with you, and I'm just not ready for it.

Me: Awww okay.

TWS: So I think it's best you didn't come.

My mouth dropped, and my heart just fucking fell on the floor.

Me: Ok. But we can still be cool tho, right?

Wait, did I just beg this one song singing mufucka to be my friend? Tha Fuck!?

TWS: No, I just think it's best that we stop talking. You're a nice guy tho.

Me: I get it. You're right. Maybe we shouldn't be friends anymore. I agree.

TWS: I'm sorry. Take care of yourself tho, Reggie.

Me: Yeah, you too.

Man, a tear just rolled down my mufuckin' face. What the fuck just happened right here? We had plans and shit. I had Royal Blue all ready to go. Now, I gotta go unpack that shit and put that cologne I don't even remember the name of back in the cabinet.

You ever just had somebody break yo got damn heart out of the blue. It wasn't that I even liked her like that. Her reasoning just fucked me all the way up. The fucking nerve of her.

That shit made me think about all the girls in the past that said they weren't interested. Was it because of my scar? Were they embarrassed to be with me? Did they like me, and then it got to a point when they didn't want to introduce me to their friends and family, so they just ended the shit? What the fuck? What kinda friends does she have? She was too young anyway. She shallow as fuck. And her friends shallow too. Fuck her friends and fuck her too. She wasn't all that anyway.

So, I think you can tell that this fucked my whole world up. It fucked it up in a major way.

Good thing is, I'm dating other women, so I can just call one of them. Let's see who's free tonight. You know a mufucka had to have a back up. I always had back ups for shit like this. You ain't gone have my ass down too long because I had other women to pick my ass right back up. I knew exactly who to call.

I call her and she is available. I'm back in the saddle all within minutes. She is a lot prettier, and I'm sure she fucked better than The Wedding Singer would have. I turned "DMSR" back on.

Damn, this is not the right song for this moment. "DMSR" ain't doing it for me right now. I know Prince got a song for this moment, but I ain't got time to think about it, so I just turned the shit off.

We go out and have a good time. I can't remember where we went. But I remember us spending the night together and we had a good ass night. But The Wedding Singer's words were on my mind the whole time.

The next day, when I looked at my boarding pass, I got a little sad. I still shoulda gone. Why didn't I still go to Atlanta tho? Why am I just thinking about that shit as I write this? I got all kinda friends and family in Atlanta. I still could have gone and had a good ass time. Anyway, I thought about the conversation from the day before and got mad at her ass all over again. It was bout to be a long ass road.

I was dating too many women anyway. Hell, fucking her woulda just complicated shit. I'm glad she didn't want me to come. Her seeing me in Royal Blue woulda just made shit worse. Hell yeah, I was trying to make myself feel better. Not sure if it was working, but I was trying everything.

Here's what I told myself, "Reggie, the next woman you meet and you like - you're going to get serious with her and date her only. And she's going to be finer than her, have a better personality than her, cuz she wasn't all that anyway. I'm bout to show her ass."

My mind was literally all over the place. I could not gather my thoughts. All I knew was that I was hurting in that moment and would have done anything to have my cousin Tammie hold my hands and say, "It's okay cuz, you not gone fall. I got you."

THE AFTERTHOUGHT
WHAT DA FUCK THEY SAYING?

And another thing...
You know how sometimes you cuss a mufucka out on the phone, then some more shit hit you when you hang up, and you be like *Damn, I shoulda said, "And yo dick little!"* or and *"yo pussy stank!"* I didn't want to go back and edit because I don't think it would have flowed right, so this is the afterthought.

I wonder if my friends prepped people for my scars and shit. I know you're like *I don't get it.* I'm bout to explain. Say you're having a party and your loud mouth uncle or rude ass auntie is coming, so you prep the people saying, "Look, don't pay no attention to my uncle. He's an asshole, but he means well, or, "Don't pay no attention to my auntie. She just be talking shit, or "My friend Sheila is coming. She's a little bougie, but she cool tho."

I've always wondered what descriptors people used to prep others for me. Were they physical or character descriptors? Did people describe my personality, my vibe or my look? Did they say, "My boy Reggie coming. He cool as shit. He a good dude.", and leave it at that? Or did they say, "My boy Reggie coming, he got burned and got a crippled hand, but the nigga cool as hell." What do people say? You ever wonder how people describe you behind your back? Well shit, I did.

The Wedding Singer not wanting her friends to meet me made me think about all kinda shit. Not just about women I dated, but the regular folks in my life. It just had me questioning all of that.

When she told me she didn't want me to meet her friends because she wasn't ready to explain me, it confirmed the shit I'd always wondered or thought. I had always felt people mentioned my burn when they described me or didn't take me around others because of it, and she confirmed all that shit. So my feelings and thoughts about it were real. It's kinda like you've been cut, but you don't even feel the shit or react to it til you see the blood. Well, she showed me the blood, so now I felt the cut AND saw the blood. And it didn't feel good. I'm not sure if it was the words that hurt or the confirmation of it all. Either way, I didn't like the feeling.

I processed and dealt with her words for a long time. Those words and the confirmation of it all stuck with me for some years. I mean, years. That was some hard shit to shake off because the scars weren't going anywhere. So that meant it was going to always be this way and that I had to figure this shit out.

Some years later I was dating this girl, and I asked her if people stared at me when we were out together. She said they stared all the time. I was shocked.

I was like, "Really?! Why don't you tell me when you see them stare? What do you do when you see them staring at me?"

She said, "I stare back at them mufuckas and give them the 'What the fuck you looking at' look. I be bout to beat they ass."

I just laughed, fist bumped her and said, "You my mufucka!" That was a cool moment.

It was then that I realized that if you're with me, you have to handle the stares and the crazy looks for me when I don't see them. You gotta be able to get a mufucka off me when I'm not looking. You gotta be just as strong or stronger than me, for me. We gotta be that shit for each other. So The Wedding Singer wasn't strong enough to be with me. *That's* what it is. I need a Gangsta Bitch.

CHAPTER 8
CIRCLING BACK

It's early 2013, and I'm standing on the balcony of the downtown apartment my wife and I are renting. It's on the 13th floor and has a really cool view. I'm standing out here with a glass of single malt scotch and a cigar. Single malt is my shit. I'm thinking, *This ain't the life I'm supposed to be living. I don't know what it is, but this ain't.*

My wife and I have a successful laundry delivery service. Financially, we are good. But something is missing. I ain't supposed to be in Dallas. I'm supposed to be doing something else with my life. I'm 40 years old, doing shit that I don't wanna do, and time is running out. I'm so unhappy, it's ridiculous. I'm supposed to be on somebody's stage speaking and inspiring people. Wait a minute, nigga! Who can you inspire when you're not even happy your damn self? Who can you inspire and you're not even doing what you wanna be doing? You're not even speaking your own truth. You're not even living your own truth. What, you gone get on stage and talk about being broken? Yeah right! Sit yo ass down somewhere. I poured the glass of scotch out over the balcony, used the water hose to put the cigar out, and thought to myself, *I really don't even like cigars - fake ass nigga.* Then, I walked back inside.

I know you're like, *Damn, we didn't even get the wedding.* I know because this book aint bout my marriage. That's a whole different story with a whole different message - trust me. You may get that later; you may not. But those years I was married deserves a whole book. And this aint the book.

I started doing some serious soul searching. I began this quest for my truth. My truth meaning - living my truth. Speaking my truth. Being my truth. No matter what it looked like. I needed to be honest about what I wanted. The first person I thought about was The Wedding Singer. I didn't say everything I needed to say to her. I had some shit I needed to get off my chest. I no longer had her phone number because she was the last person I wanted to talk to for years. So I looked for her on LinkedIN - nothing. Googled her - nothing. Then I went to Facebook- VOILA! There she was.

I sent her a friend request, and she accepted. For about two weeks, I just stalked her page trying to see if I could get an idea of what had been going on in her life. I saw that she was married. I saw she had a beautiful little girl. They were a cute family. She looked happy. But who looks sad on social media? Finally, I'd had enough of the stalking shit and sent her a message. I asked her if we could talk, and she said yes. I couldn't wait. I asked for her phone number and called within seconds of getting it.

Me: Heeyyy you!

She was puzzled as fuck.

Wedding Singer: Uhh Hey.

Me: So how are things? How are you? Long time.

Still puzzled as fuck.

Wedding Singer: They're okay. I'm well. You?

Still puzzled as fuck.

Me: Look, I've been looking for you for a while. I got something I wanna say to you.

Wedding Singer: I'm sure you do. I was actually looking for you too.

Me: I wanna say thank you.

Still puzzled as fuck.

Wedding Singer: Thank you?

Me: Yeah, thank you.

Wedding Singer: You sure you called the right person? Hahaha.

Me: Hahaha. Yeah, I'm sure

Wedding Singer: I'm sure you were calling to call me cuss me out after the way I treated you. But you wanna *thank* me?

Me: Nah, I don't wanna cuss you out. I wanna thank you because I'm starting this journey to Reggie - this journey to being honest about being who I am, and I thought about you.

When you told me years ago that you couldn't handle explaining me, you couldn't handle how your friends would perceive me - that was honest. It was fucked up for me to have to hear that, but at the time, that was your truth and you spoke it. And you stood by it. You knew what you could and couldn't handle and I appreciate you telling me the truth and not making for an awkward visit. To me, that's an example of living your truth. So thank you. And that's what I wanna do. Be honest about how I feel.

Wedding Singer: Damn. That's some grown ass shit. I've been thinking about you for years. How I needed to reach out to you and apologize and here you are thanking me. So not what I expected.

Me: I know.

Wedding Singer: Reggie, I was so wrong. I was so shallow. I know I was all kinda bitches.

Me: Yeah you were. Hahaha.

Wedding Singer: Hahaha. I'm sure. Will you forgive me?

Me: Of course. So how you been?

Wedding Signer: No Nigga! How YOU been? Hahaha.

She still had that cool personality and sense of humor. We finished the conversation on a high note. I applauded her for being able to speak her truth at such a young age. We laughed, shared smiles and other life happenings. It was a good time. We remained Facebook friends. We would comment and laugh on each other's posts from time to time.

In my mind, she was trustworthy. I knew she was somebody that wouldn't lie to me. When I look back, she was actually gentle with her delivery. I respect her for that. I'm not even sure if forgiving her was even necessary. But I did since she asked for it. Maybe she needed that to go on with her life. Because what did she really do? She told her truth and it hurt my feelings. She confirmed some shit I was already thinking. So, I guess the truth does hurt sometimes.

Yeah, it took me years to get over it, but I don't think she should apologize for how something made me feel. I think people should apologize for their actions, not for how people respond to them. People can't control others' reaction or response to what they do. So how can they apologize for it? But people can apologize for the shit they did to cause that reaction or response. People argue about that scenario all the time. So moving on. In my mind, The Wedding Singer was no longer a simple bitch. But she coulda at least gave my money back for my ticket tho haha.

I went on tour in 2018. She came to my show in Atlanta and sat right in the front row. It was hella cool to see her. We both smiled so big when we saw each other. After the show we hugged tight and long. I swear it was one of the most honest and refreshing hugs ever. It was like that call on that Tuesday afternoon never happened, but it did.

Maybe she was a Gangsta Bitch after all.

CHAPTER 9
I AM NOT OKAY

My mama always got some shit for me to do - clean this, move this, hang this, fix this, go get me a Pepsi, "Hey get me some Popeyes on your way home." - I'm always doing something. And I never get tired of it. I go to the Bluff from Dallas every three or four months just to do shit. I swear, I clean the same junk out of the same room every time I go home. I be like, "Damn, did she hire a mufucka to put this same shit back in here when I left? Did she hire a mufucka to put these same holes back in the wall after I patched them up? ...tha fuck is going on here?"

Whenever I'm doing what she's asked me to do, she'll peek her head in, "Reg what's going on in here? What are you doing in here? You ok?" I be like, "Umm I'm doing the shit you told me to do." I mean, I don't say "shit" but you get what I'm saying. "Yes, Mama I'm okay." She always makes sure I'm hydrated, and my tummy is full. Sometimes, I'll be doing some shit and look around and see a random bottle of water, a piece of candy or a napkin with some cookies sitting there. I just shake my head, drink the water, fuck the cookies up and finish the task. Oh, I fucking love cookies. Just thought I'd let y'all know that.

Okay back to what I was saying.

I normally go home, knock out whatever it is she has me to do in two to three days and she always says, "You did that fast."

At some point during the visit we always eat some pizza from Big Banjo and watch a movie - some kinda drama or suspense. That's her shit. My ass always falls asleep on the couch while we watch the movie. I wake up in the middle of the night sitting in the dark on the couch. That's our normal shit.

Then I head back to Dallas.

It's been about eight months since I had found the Wedding Singer and reconnected with her. I was in the Bluff on one of my visits. I came home to clean out my old childhood bedroom. A lot of my old shit was still in there. I had a lot of shit on the walls - some Prince album covers, some Run DMC albums covers and posters, some old pictures of LL, Big Daddy Kane, New Edition, Salt 'n Pepa, Shirley Murdock ole cheating ass, Sheila E, Vesta and a whole bunch of other folks. I cannot say Vesta's name without hitting "Congratulations" or at least humming the shit. I was bout to ask y'all to sing that shit with me but now ain't the time haha. Rest in Peace, Vesta. Okay, so my room still had the same red, white, and blue striped wallpaper it had on there when I was a lil dude. So I gotta take that shit down too.

This shouldn't take any time - two days tops.

On my fourth day, I took a box from my bedroom to the living room. As I was sitting it down, Moms peeked her thru the kitchen door.

Moms: Reg, you moving a little slower than normal. Are you okay?

I rose up. Took a deep breath. My eyes watered.

Me: No Mama, I'm not okay.

She grew concerned.

Moms: Well Reggie, what's wrong.

Me: Mama, me and Shonda getting a divorce.

Moms: Why? Is it another woman?

I just shook my head as a tear rolled down my face.

Me: No it's not.

Moms: Well, is it another man?

Me: No, not that I know of.

Moms: Well, talk to me. What is it, Reggie?

Me: Mama, I'm not sure. I just know I'm not happy.

Moms: Happy with what?

Me: Me. I'm not doing what I'm supposed to be doing. I supposed to be doing more.

Moms: What do you think you're supposed to be doing, Babe?

Me: I'm supposed to be traveling the world telling my story. I have an amazing story and I'm supposed to be telling it. My story is supposed to be inspiring people.

Moms: Hm. Okay.

Me: God left me here for a reason, Mama. I'm not doing what I'm supposed to be doing. All the stuff I've been thru. I think I turned out okay with all I've been through.

Moms: You know Reggie, I know you've been thru a lot. I've always prayed that with everything that happened, you would be okay and nothing would stop you and that you would turn out to be a good man. And I think God heard me because you turned out to be a good person. You're a good man, and I'm proud of you.

Me: Thanks Mama, I've been thru so much and the world needs to hear it. I've gotten past soooo much and I still made it.

Moms: Well, can you tell me some of the stuff you been thru?

Me: All the people picking on me. All the name calling. All the jokes. All the laughing at me. And I still made it. People need to hear about that.

Moms: Picking on you?!?! Wait, when did they pick on you?

Me: When I was growing up.

Moms: What?!!! What did they say?

Me: Called me burnt pig. Talked about my head when I was going thru surgery. Talked about my hand and my face.

Called me all kinda names. They did this all my life, and I still made it.

Moms: When did they do all this, and why didn't you tell me?

Me: When I was growing up cuz Daddy told me I couldn't run to y'all every time somebody said something because I wouldn't be strong. I thought he woulda told you.

She got really quiet and her eyes watered.

Moms: Mm. No he didn't. So what did you do when they said all this?

Now I'm crying a little more.

Me: Sometimes I'd beat they ass or sometimes I just went in my room, cried, prayed, and went back outside.

Moms: I'm your mama. How did I not know this? Hmph, how did I not know you were going through all of this. Hmph.

Me: I had gotten really good at keeping it to myself and just dealing with it. Trust me, you wouldn't have known.

Moms: Well, Reggie, how are you dealing with that now - the people picking on you?

Me: I'm fine now. It doesn't bother me anymore.

Moms: You sure? Would you tell me?

Me: Yeah, I would.

Moms: You can tell me anything. I hate you went through that. But if you say you're okay, I'm going to trust you.

Me: I'm good, Mama.

Moms: Okay, I won't keep asking.

Moms: I wish you woulda told me. But, I understand.

Me: See Mama. I got a purpose. I've been thru a lot. God has given me a purpose. And what I'm supposed to do, LaShonda is not supposed to go with me.

Moms: I really love LaShonda, but I actually understand. I get what you're saying. Hmph. Come over here. Let's sit down.

We sat on the couch right next to each other and held hands.

Me: Mama, are you doing what you wanted to do with your life? Are you doing what you were supposed to do? Is being a teacher what you wanted to do? Are you living the life you wanted to?

Mama: Yeah, it is. I never wanted the city or anything. Pine Bluff was always the perfect size for me. I like it. And when I was growing up, all I ever wanted to do was teach kids. I wanted to make a difference in little kids' lives. So I'm doing exactly what I want to do. I love it. It's been great doing it. So I understand you saying you're not doing what you want to do. I want you to be happy. If y'all can work it out - great cuz I think she's awesome. But if y'all can't, I get that too. I just want you happy. And I'm sure you'll do what you feel is best.

Me: Mama, I've never heard it from you, but can you tell me what happened to me? Can you tell me how everything happened?

Mama: Well, you were a baby. You were like one month old. You were sleep in your bassinet at your Big Mama's house. And I wanted to take me a quick shower while you were sleep. So I tried to rush and take me a shower and when I got out, the house was on fire.

Me: How did it start?

Mama: They said it was electrical but I always felt like your bassinet was too close to that gas heater on the wall. I think your sheets caught on fire from that. Do you remember those heaters at Big Mama's house?

Me: Yes ma'am, I do. Who got me out the fire?

Mama: Me and Mr. Downs from across the street got you out.

Me: Did anyone else get burned?

Mama: No, it was just you.

Me: Man, Mama you were just 20 years old. You were a kid yourself.

Mama: Hmmm. Yeah, I guess I was.

Me: See Mama, I want to tell my story and help people be themselves in spite of what happened to them. I want people to be free of their past. That's why I say I'm left here for a bigger purpose.

Mama: Yeah, I guess you are. Well if that's what you think God wants you to do, I think that's exactly what you should do.

Me: Oh, you better believe it. That's what a nigga bout to do. Hahaha ,and I'm gone kill 'em

Mama: Hahaha, I know you will. I love you.

Me: I love you too, Mama.

We gave each other a really tight hug. I kissed her on the cheek and I got up to finish cleaning out my old shit. She sat there for a little while longer.

I'd heard other versions of what happened, but this was the first time I heard my mom's. I feel like it was an abbreviated version but that may be all she allowed herself to remember or talk about. I wish I would have asked more questions. But I think that she told me all she had the strength or memory to tell. At a moment like that, I don't think she would have held anything back. So I'm good with her version of what happened.

This moment made me realize I had some work to do - some healing to do. I needed some help and some answers about myself that I couldn't even get from my mom. And that was fine. Because I'm gone get to the bottom of this shit.

I had always thought my mom settled by teaching in the Bluff for forty years. I had always wanted more for her. What is more tho? I had no fucking idea. But hell, she was doing exactly what she wanted to do in the city she wanted to be in. Well damn. Who am I to say what a person should be doing with their lives, especially my mama? I needed to sit my ass down somewhere. How cool is that to know that your mom was actually living her dream. I love that shit. Now it was time for me to do the same!

I guess that explains her wearing the big ass shades wherever she goes, even inside the mall. I guess she was like, "Bitch I'm out here living my dream. Tha fuck you think this is!"

Gone Mama! Wit yo bad ass!

I'd like to think that trip was more than just me getting old shit out of my bedroom. I was getting some old feelings and questions out as well. Normally I would kinda blow it off when she would ask me if I was okay while doing shit. I'd be like, "Duh, why wouldn't I be?" But this time, I'm glad she peeked around the corner and asked, "You okay?" Because I wasn't. And her ass was right there. Myyy Nigga.

CHAPTER 10
FIRST DAY OF THERAPY

A few weeks after I cleaned out my room, I decided it was time. It was fall 2013, and I remember when I first walked in the therapy room. All I'm going to say is, I heard some fucking pins drop. Yeah, it was that quiet. It was calmly decorated. On the left side of the room, there was a yellow, gray and white love seat next to an end table with a lit lamp and a little green plant. In the middle of the floor was a small solid colored round rug. On the right side of the room were two chairs with a floor lamp to the right of them. On the wall, there were a couple random pics of nature and her degrees. You know, as I type this, I never saw where she got her degrees or certifications from. I always check this type of shit out. Whenever I'm waiting on the doctor, my nosy ass will lean over their desk to see where they got their shit from. I need to know. I need to make sure you're equipped to handle the shit I'm going through. Funny, but I didn't lean over to see if she was legit.

There was not one couch in sight. I was expecting a couch, so I could lay my feet up on the arm of the mufucka. In every movie I've ever watched that had a therapist, there was a couch when a mufucka went to therapy, and she didn't have one. Oh shit, she ain't real. I shoulda leaned over to see her degrees to see if she was real. Fuck! I wanted a couch, and she ain't got no fucking couch. This bout to be a long road.

I walked in and sat in one of the two chairs and waited patiently til she came in.

Reggie, what the fuck are you bout to say to this woman whom you've never met? A woman who doesn't know shit about you? A *white* woman at that. I knew she was white because she had a little profile pic on the website advertising therapists in my area, and she was close to the crib. I needed a mufucka that I could get to quickly before I changed my damn mind. I didn't know shit about choosing a damn therapist. Anyway, *what are you bout to say to this white woman, Reggie? What you gone tell her?*

If you've ever been to therapy, you might know what I'm feeling. It's kinda like when you're sitting on the edge of that lil exam table with that paper on it at the doc's office. You know how you sit there and dangle ya feet til the nurse or medical assistant walks in to check your blood pressure and shit. Well, it's kinda like that. Or when the doctor's office calls you to tell you that the doctor saw something in your bloodwork, they don't tell you what it is over the phone, so you need to come in person to get the news. Yo ass be like, *Oh shit, what they bout to tell me?* Well it was like that for me.

    I heard the door open. I got nervous as hell. Aww shit, it was time.

    She walked in. She had short white hair. She was wearing a little yellow sweater, some slacks, and holding a cup of something steaming hot. Damn, was she matching her office decorations? She had on some cool black rimmed glasses. She was carrying a little notepad and a dark colored ink pen. She appeared to be in her mid to late sixties. She looked like somebody's auntie. She had a real calming disposition, I might add. She closed the door behind her and sat down slowly on the loveseat. She smiled slightly and looked me dead in my eyes. I love when people give me eye contact.

    "Good morning, Reggie. My name is Patricia but you can call me Pat. So tell me what brings you here today?"

    I had no idea where to start with answering that question. I sat there in silence for a couple seconds. She just kinda smirked while I sat there. I was even asking myself, *Yeah Reggie, why are you here?* I just told my wife of seven years I can't do this no more. She had no idea it was coming. Hell, neither did I. I was confused. I was feeling all types of ways. I was feeling unaccomplished, broken, lost, hurt, guilty, angry, with no direction...a whole bunch of shit. Name some more bad shit - I was feeling that shit too.

"Good morning Pat. I'm fucked up and I need help. That's what brings me here today."

That may have been the first time I said that shit out loud to somebody other than myself. It felt weird as fuck hearing it. But y'all remember when I said "Pops Boy" told me I was following in my dad's footsteps and how it triggered me to quit my job? I really think saying and hearing shit out loud gets me to move on shit.

She took a sip of her hot drink and said, "What do you mean you're fucked up? What does fucked up mean?"

Wait, did she just ask me to tell her what I mean by that shit? She wasn't just going to take me at my word? She's going to make me describe the shit. Is she challenging me right now? Okay Pat, I see what's going on here.

I didn't feel like picking and choosing my words, so I said, "Pat, can I talk how I talk?"

She said, "By all means, please do."

I was bout to let her ass have it.

"It means I'm hurting. I got some issues. I keep hurting people. I've been hurt by some people. I'm scared to talk about my problems to people. I'm not living the life that I really want to live. Everything I'm living is a lie. I'm unhappy as fuck. I'm not doing what I really want to be doing. I get up every morning and do some shit that I don't like. I'm not who I want to be. I thought my life would be a lot different. I fucking hate this city. I want to be somewhere else. I want to move. But something is keeping me here. But I don't even know where I really want to go. I keep lying to people. I don't like myself right now. No, actually I hate myself right now. I'm not sure if I ever really liked myself. I hate that I got burned. I hate my hand. I hate my face. One week ago, I moved out of the house with my wife on our anniversary. The look on her face killed me, and I still left. How could I just leave someone like that? She didn't deserve that shit. She didn't deserve none of the shit I did to her. I cheated on her time and time again. I hate myself for that. I'm tired of being the person I am."

I said a few more things. But I started repeating myself, and I started crying. I couldn't believe I was telling all of this to a white woman that looks like the ultimate white auntie. I didn't even know if she was legit, and I didn't even know her. But that was the beauty of it - she didn't fucking know me and I didn't know her ass either. So just maybe she wouldn't judge me - hell I wouldn't have cared if she did.

I cried for about a minute. It was like I needed that shit. I actually felt a little better. Damn, was a weight just lifted? Okay cool, session is over, I'm done. Maybe a nigga just needed to cry.

Pat let me get the cry out. She just sat there. She looked at me like what I had just told her was nothing. I was thinking, *Wait, did you just hear all the shit I just said? Yo ass ain't got nothing to say?*

"So if your life wasn't 'fucked up' *(She did the little air quotes thing. I love when people do that because I can't. I try, but yeah, my fingers won't let me be great. So I knew we were bout to get along)* how do you think it would look?"

"Well, I'd be happy. I would have never gotten burned. I would have never lied to all those women. I would have never cheated on my wife. Hell ,I probably wouldn't have married her so soon, to be honest. I think I would have waited. Shit - I know I would have waited. I wouldn't be in Dallas. I would probably be in Chicago or New York. I would have a kid by now."

Pat just sat there and let me ramble. She never interrupted me. She would let me finish. And every time I did, she would ask me another simple ass question about something I said and my ass would start to ramble all over again. I think that entire session was me just rambling. She probably asked me four damn questions the entire session. Wait, you're charging me $125 per hour to just ask me some simple ass questions? Nah see, this is why I should have leaned over the desk to see where she got her degrees from.

Pat asked these simple ass questions that got me to admit to and answer some hard shit. She was getting me to open up. She was getting me to say shit out loud and that made it real. I was being honest about shit. Shit that I'd thought about before but would never say to anybody. I wouldn't say the shit because I would either be too embarrassed, I wasn't ready to say it, or I thought it would make me look weak or damaged. I'll be damned if you gone have me out here in these Dallas streets looking weak and damaged. But I definitely would do it with White Auntie Pat behind closed doors.

Well damn.

Looking back, this was simple shit to White Auntie Pat. I'm sure she'd heard worse. Smh.

She looked at her watch and said we needed to start wrapping up because I only had a few more minutes and she wanted to go over a few things. Damn, I could do this all day. I was getting into this shit. I was like, *Ask me some more shit.* It was like the movie was just getting good, and then it ended. No White Auntie Pat, let's keep going.

So the first session was different for me. I'd never done anything like that before. I must say, I felt lighter. My tears dried up before the session ended.

During her wrap up, she told me she wanted me to get a journal and start writing down everything - good thoughts, bad thoughts, happy thoughts, things I did that day, things I thought about that day. Talk about how the day started and how it ended. Ask myself did the day go how I wanted it to? Did it end like I wanted to? If it didn't, was there anything I could have done to get the desired ending. Just a whole bunch of shit.

She said she'd be interested to see what I'd write about, and when I returned she wanted me to read my shit out loud. I was like, *Whoa, you want me to read my shit out loud? Okay, you asked for it White Auntie Pat.*

Before I left, she asked me when I wanted to come back. I was like, "Shit, when is your next available appointment?" It was in three days. I was like, "Fuck it, I'll take it." This was day one and the shit was already fun for me. I was getting to talk about all this shit I had bottled up, and she wasn't even flinching. I loved this shit.

I walked to my car smiling hella hard. I was like, *Damn, she is so cool.* I immediately went to Target and bought four damn notebooks. I knew I had a lot to write about. I had a lot to say. I was ready to journal my day. I kept that shit with me. I started carrying a backpack everywhere to keep my journals in just in case I needed to stop and write some shit down. If you saw me, you saw my ass with a backpack.

One time, I went to the crib to visit Moms and everywhere we went I had my backpack. We went to Walmart - backpack. Popeye's - backpack. Dillards - backpack. She said "What's up with this backpack? I've never seen you carry a backpack. That's some white boy shit. White boys carry backpacks. When you start doing that shit? What you got in there?" I said, "Just a bunch of personal stuff."

I had to be able to just stop and jot my thoughts down because random shit would trigger all types of thoughts throughout the day, and I didn't want to forget that shit by the time I got home. So, I had to have access to my journal at all times because I never knew when some shit would hit me.

So I was writing my ass off. Thinking my ass off. I was writing down all types of shit in my journal. I would be like, "...and at 1:06 a bug landed on my right arm and I smashed the mufucka. He had me fucked up." I was detailed as fuck with my journaling. It was a good way for me to chronicle my day. I didn't realize how much shit I thought about on the regular. And at the end of the day, I would light a candle and write some more to reflect on my day. I loved the things she told me to write about. I talked about how my day went versus how I wanted it to go, just like she recommended. Some days went just like I wanted them to. Some days didn't. I even talked about things I could have done differently to get the desired outcome, just like she recommended.

I started setting realistic expectations for myself. This style of journaling began to make me more accountable and responsible for my day. It also made me look back at my day to better prepare for the next day. Damn, all this in just a few days of journaling. I got addicted to the shit. I couldn't wait to get back to Auntie Pat to read my shit out loud.

The shit was going to be fun because I have always loved reading aloud. When the teacher called on me to read in elementary school, I did that shit with no problem. I was eager to read aloud. For one, I wanted to show off my reading skills because I went to a school with some horrible reading mufuckas. I would be like "Mrs. Terrell, can we get somebody else to read cuz this mufucka is fucking these words up." Nah, I wouldn't say that, but I'd be thinking it tho. I was a reading snob. But nobody knew that shit. For two, I liked hearing myself read. I read plenty of books to myself as a child, so it was going to be nice to read my own shit to somebody else.

I didn't really know what to expect from all this therapy shit. But I knew I was at a point where I just wanted to be honest about what I was feeling, what I was going through, what I had been through, and what I wanted with my life. And I just wanted to talk to someone. I felt like there was a lot of shit suppressed and it needed to at least come out. I didn't know what was going to happen when the shit came out. I just knew I wanted it out.

When I was home a few weeks earlier cleaning out my old bedroom, I asked my moms what she was going to do with all my old stuff and what she was going to put in my room. She said, "I don't know yet. I'll probably just have you put it on the curb for the trash man. And I don't know what I'm going to put in there yet. I just know I want that old stuff outta there." So, I guess therapy was going to be like cleaning out my old bedroom for me. I was going to take all the old shit out to the curb for the trash man, so I can have some space for some new shit.

The next therapy session was going to be bomb. I was looking forward to it. I had a lot to talk about.

I guess you can say Auntie Pat was legit.

CHAPTER 11
ANOTHER THERAPY SESSION

I drove to my second session with a big ass smile on my face. I couldn't wait to talk about all the shit I had written. I parked the car, grabbed my backpack and damn near sprinted into the building. Spoke to every mufucka I passed by. *Hello everybody, I'm on my way to therapy to read my shit.*

When I got inside, I saw Auntie Pat standing in the hall. She had on an outfit similar to the one she had on last time, and she still had on those cool ass glasses. She was making a cup of coffee. She asked me if I wanted one. I wasn't the biggest coffee drinker, but this felt like a coffee moment, so fuck it, I had one.

She directed me to the little therapy room. I sat there and waited for a minute or two before she walked in with her little notepad and ink pen. She asked a few get to know you questions. I realized, then, that I hadn't told her where I was from, how old I was, or anything like that during the last session. When I told her I was originally from Pine Bluff, Arkansas she got excited because she was also from a small town in Arkansas. I didn't give her a chance to ask that type of shit last time since I just unloaded on her ass when I said "I'm fucked up. Can you help me?" So, I guess you can say we were breaking the ice.

She asked me if I had a chance to do my homework assignment. I picked up my journal and flipped through about 40-50 pages and said, "Does it look like I did my homework?" She laughed and said, "GREAT! Looks like you had a lot of shit to talk about. I doubt we get through all of that today, but let's see what you got." I loved the fact that she was a cusser. I'd like to think that I made her feel like it was okay to cuss because I cussed my ass off in the first session.

I started reading my journal entries. I wish I could remember exactly what I read about, but I'd be lying if I said I did. But I remember her laughing at some of the shit, taking notes, looking over the top of her black rimmed glasses and asking me a couple follow up questions that made me dig a little deeper, be clearer, or explore a different perspective. I was loving this shit. I was getting so much out of my system. Good days and bad days. Saying it out loud was helping me push it out and talk about it. Hearing it was doing something too. Hearing about my own day was interesting. I began to think, *Reggie, you a crazy mufucka, and you low key funny.* She was laughing her ass off at some of the stuff. At the other stuff she would just write a note and hit me with a question. Or just sit there.

After I read some of my shit, she said "Damn, you did write a lot and you gave a lot of details." Then, she asked me what I got out of the assignment. I told her it was interesting to hear about my day, and that maybe I shouldn't write so many details, but it was fun. It was relaxing, and it felt refreshing to just get shit out my system and talk about it. I also told her that I needed to get a damn life, hahaha. She suggested doing it again, and I said that was no problem. We scheduled our next appointment for the following week. I was just as excited, maybe even more, to do this shit again.

I closed my little journal, put it in my backpack, and I was outta there.

When I got home, I did the same thing that I did before. I lit a candle and started writing. After doing this for some days, I noticed I started talking about all types of shit. Not just the shit that happened during the day, but other shit I was thinking about. I was really getting into this shit. I started talking about my dreams and shit. I was like, *Damn, this shit is cool.* I wrote down how I'd always wanted to live out of RV for a year and travel the country. I wrote down how I hated what I was doing for a living but that it made money. At the time, I owned a laundry pick up and delivery service. I hated that shit, but it was hella profitable. I started talking about jobs and shit I hated in the past and what I saw myself doing in the future. Damn, this was getting deep.

When it was time to go back to my session, I was excited as usual. This time, because I had some more substantial shit to talk about. Well, it seemed more substantial. I mean, I had the everyday shit, but now, I was talking about dreams and goals.

I remember when I told Auntie Pat that I wanted to live in an RV for a year and just travel the country, she asked, "Did somebody tell you that you couldn't do it?"

I said "No."

She asked, "Well, what's keeping you from doing it?"

I said that nothing was.

Then she said, "Hm, if you were to do it, describe how you think it would be."

Man, I went off.

I said, "The shit would be cool, freeing, relaxing. I would just stop in random towns, get random odd jobs, meet random people, jog everyday. I wouldn't even take a map. I would just drive in the direction I wanted to go. I would let the sun and the moon guide me. I would park at rest tops and stick my feet out the window and wiggle my toes. Go fishing. That's just some of the shit I would do."

She laughed and said, "That sounds like fun. So you're a wanderlust. There are people who do shit like that. And they are some of the happiest people."

She told me about some guy to look up, but I forgot his name. Then she suggested I start writing down the things that made me feel good and to do more of those things. Before I left, we just went ahead and got me on a regular schedule to see her.

We started talking about all types of shit during my sessions. She would even tell me little tidbits about herself. She was cool.

One day, I said something about my burn and she asked me how it happened. It was like she was just waiting on a good way to bring it up but wanted me to bring it up first. I told her it happened when I was one month old at my grandmother's house in Louisville, MS. She expressed a little sympathy but didn't sit in that shit long. I think she could tell I didn't need sympathy. She asked me about how it made me feel, how it affected my life, what I thought of the burns, if anyone else got burned, and all types of questions that my answers prompted.

I told her they made me feel like I was different. I always got crazy looks. People looked weirded out or jerked when they shook my hand. So I would always just keep it in my pocket just to avoid people's stares. I was the only one that got burned to my knowledge. I wasn't quite sure how the fire started. I'd heard a couple versions aside from the version I had just heard from my moms.

I told her about the moment in the caf on the Yard. She took a few notes and asked me what all my father said. I told her how he had warned me that the world was going to be cruel and what to say the next time someone insulted me because of my burn. He encouraged me to be tough and strong - what tough and strong meant. It meant I had to handle the shit and not show weakness and not run to him or my mama every time I was hurt.

Auntie Pat: Did someone ever say it to you again?

Me: Of course.

Auntie Pat: How did you feel when they said it?

Me: Shit, it hurt. I was mad.

She wrote some shit down.

Auntie Pat: Did you run to him or your mom?

Me: Nooo! Hell no.

Auntie Pat: What did you do?

I shrugged my shoulders.

Me: I would just go in my room and cry. I just dealt with it.

Auntie Pat: So you didn't talk to anyone about it?

Me: Nah.

Auntie Pat: Hm. So you didn't talk about it. You just dealt with it. And how old were you again when this happened?

Me: I was eight.

Auntie Pat: How old was your dad? Do you remember?

Me: He's 21 years older than me. I guess he was about 29 or 30. Wait, it was the summer. So he was 30.

Auntie Pat: Aw okay. He was a young guy. Did you ever tell anybody? You just went in your room and cried.

Me: Nope. I just went to my room and cried.

Auntie Pat: Would you say you've been keeping quiet and dealing with this on your own since you were eight?

I got quiet as fuck. She just sat there til I answered.

Me: I guess you can say that. Yeah, I guess you can say that.

Auntie Pat: Hm. That's a lot for an eight year old.

Me: Yeah, I guess it is.

Auntie Pat: I don't want to put words in your mouth. But would you say you shut down?

Me: Damn. I guess I did, huh.

Auntie Pat: I think that's shutting down. You didn't talk to anybody. You got quiet and just cried to yourself. Hm.

Me: Yeah, I guess that is shutting down.

Auntie Pat: How old are you again?

Me: I just turned 41.

Auntie Pat: Hm. That's a long time. Well, you can talk here. Okay.

Me: Yes ma'am.

Auntie Pat: Do you pray?

Me: Yes ma'am.

Auntie Pat: Ok.

Damn. Did Auntie Pat just make realize I shut down and have been quiet for 31 damn years. Wow. Just wow. She asked a few more questions. I asked if we could change the subject. She was cool with it.

That realization was a bit much. I didn't realize how I had been pretty much keeping quiet for that damn long. I had been holding in feelings and dealing with shit on my own since I was fucking eight years old - not going to anybody, not even my parents. That's a long fucking time.

I went home and wrote all this shit down. I thought about all the relationships I had been in with women saying I didn't really communicate well, I didn't come to them, and I didn't let them in. I thought letting someone in was telling them how I got burned or what happened to me. Apparently, there was more to it than that. Hell, I guess I didn't know how to, now that I think about it. I've been running off to be by myself to deal with my problems since I was eight. Shit, what else do you expect me to do?

Damn, no wonder I've been walking around sad as fuck on the inside. That was a lot of shit to keep bottled in. That was a lot of years of pain trapped inside of me. Damn.

So basically I fucking shut down when I was eight. SMH. Damn, that explains a lot.

I was quiet for a day or two after this session. I don't think I talked to anybody. I had to deal with that shit. That was a lot to unveil. I needed some quiet time to process this shit. I needed to just sit with it.

I thought about how Auntie Pat would question me. When she would ask me about previous experiences she had me describe what I saw, what I felt during those moments, to look at those experiences from all sides, and then pretty much summarize them. And I was saying all this shit out loud. Well, damn! I was starting to do this shit even when I was by myself. I was starting to question myself in that same way. I was starting to journal that way. Man, I was starting to process shit differently. Okay Auntie Pat, I see what you doing!

This is getting heavy, but I'm in it now, so I gotta keep going. Shit, what is Auntie Pat going to make me realize the next session? Damn.

CHAPTER 12
I'M MAD

I went home and started writing more and more. I wrote down a bunch of shit I wanted to say to people, especially the little dude at the back of the line that yelled "You fat burnt finger pig" and the dude at the back of the class that blurted out "This nigga look like he got two heads." who ended my family vacations and all my Jheri curl dreams. Fuck him too!

I had thought about those moments several times since they happened, but I had never actually wrote the shit down. That felt different. It was almost upsetting. I could see myself in line at the caf again. I could see myself in the classroom again. I could hear the kids laughing all over again. I couldn't wait to get back to see Auntie Pat. I needed her to hear the shit I had written. I felt like she would join in with me as I said, "Fuck you" out loud to these niggas. It's nothing like having someone join hands with you and saying, "Fuck you."

I even thought about times I wanted to tell somebody I was hurting but didn't. I thought about all the times I cried to myself while praying at the foot of my bed.

I went back to the fight I had with myself in the street when my pops left. I really wanted him to stay. I felt like he should have just known that without me saying anything. I thought that was a given. Hell, he was my dude. Apparently I needed to say it tho. But I was too busy being me, ole quiet ass Reg. And too busy being tough.

I thought about how I wanted to cuss The Wedding Singer out, but didn't. Yeah, we made up, but still. There were some things I wanted to say. I really wanted to cuss her ass out when she told me she didn't want to fuck with me because of my burns.

Please don't think those three moments were the only times I got picked on. There were plenty of other times, but some of those, I just blew off because they didn't quite sting like the moments I told you about. Those other times were when I fought a mufucka or just joned their ass out. I had become a master at that shit. I could say some shit to hurt your feelings and make you wanna fight. I could get you off me with my words or my hands. It didn't make a difference how you came; I would come back harder. I would get real personal too. I wouldn't just talk about the physical shit - that was too typical and expected. I would get under the skin. Talk about how you felt or your family. I would hit you on some emotional and mental shit because I had plenty of experience with it. I could size you up and imagine how you felt when you were by yourself - *that* was the shit I would say.

I recall one of my boys saying, "You like a master at talking about folks. Did somebody train you?" The crowd wouldn't always respond with laughter at the shit I said. They would sometimes say, "Damn you make a nigga wanna commit suicide."

Well, that was because I was going for pain, not laughs. I wasn't trying to please the crowd. I wanted you to think about it later and cry yo ass off. I wanted you to be at the foot of your bed crying like I was. So when they didn't laugh but got quiet, I knew I had the nigga on the ropes. And I would always finish them. I was a mufucka with my words. I was mad. And I was sad.

Some of this shit I wrote down in my journal. Some of this shit I just thought about and reflected on it because I was so busy reliving the moment that I couldn't stop to put pen to paper. But I knew I was going to tell Auntie Pat about it.

I drove to therapy with a different kinda anxiousness and intention this time. I was bobbing and weaving all thru traffic. *Get out the way mufuckas! I'm bout to go to therapy!*

I had my lil ole journal ready. I'm ready to read all this shit out loud.

I walked in, and Auntie Pat was at the coffee maker as usual. Damn, how many cups does she drink a day? Does she just stand by that mufucka all day? Does she have any other clients? She had on my favorite glasses. She nodded her head, looked over her glasses, smiled, touched me gently on my shoulder and told me to gone in the room and that she'd be in there in a sec.

She came in with her coffee, note pad and ink pen like usual. She sat down and we small talked a little. I appreciated the small talk time because she kinda let me in to who she was, and it gave me a chance to get into my space to tell her what I had written about.

We both had a thing for music. She even told me about how she was in a garage band in high school. Man, would she get excited when she told me about their performances! It was cute.

She knew I had a thing for snacks. She knew I loved cookies and Reeses Pieces.

Anyway, let me stay on track, hahaha.

The read aloud started.

She sat and listened while I said "fuck you" to all those niggas that hurt me who said the shit behind my back that wasn't bold enough to say it when I turned around. She didn't join in like I had anticipated, but she did smile and listen and that was enough for me.

She asked me would it have made a difference if I knew who they were now. I said maybe, but I wasn't sure, and that since they were just kids being kids, probably not. Didn't make a difference now.

I began to read the part about my father leaving to go back to school, how it made my moms cry, how I really wish he would have stayed, how I didn't ask him to stay because I was being tough, and how he left at one of the most important times in my life - my starting high school. He wasn't there for me to shave my first goatee. Yeah, my ass was rocking the goatee in the 11th grade. He wasn't there to meet my first real girlfriend and see me go to prom. He just missed a bunch of shit that I would have liked him to have at least witnessed. But nah, his ass was gone.

She wouldn't interrupt. She sat there and listened to me say all this shit while she jotted a note or two and looked over her black rimmed glasses. She was letting me have the stage. And I was taking that mufucka. She was in total silence. She stopped writing, pushed her glasses up on her face and asked:

Auntie Pat: Are you mad at your dad?

I was confused as shit.

Me: Mad? What do you mean?

Auntie Pat: I mean, are you mad he left? Are you mad he wasn't there for those things?

Never really thought if I was mad. I just knew I wanted him there and he wasn't.

Me: Damn. I never really thought about that. Why do you ask that?

Auntie Pat: Well I'm curious because you talk about how you wanted him there, and you didn't want him to leave, and he missed all those things but you never really said how you felt about him missing all of those things.

There she go getting me to dig deeper and tell her how I truly feel. I couldn't say I was mad at my dad. He's my dad. Is that a thing? Can you be mad at your parents?

Me: I mean, I missed him and wanted him there. I mean, it hurt.

Auntie Pat: I get it. Trust me, I do. But those things are your responses to him leaving, but how do you feel about him? What feelings do you have towards him?

Me: Damn.

I sat there for a second and a tear rolled out my eye. Auntie Pat just watched me and didn't say a word like usual.

Me: Yeah. I am mad. I'm real mad. That mufucka left me. Fuck yeah, I'm mad. He could have stayed. He just drove off and left me. Fuck him.

I was crying real tears at this point. I was wiping my face.

She kept pushing her glasses up on her face. Auntie Pat had a sadness in her eyes, but she kept a straight face.

I had never said I was mad at my parents before. Not even behind their backs. You're not supposed to be mad at your parents - not Black parents. You might get yo ass beat for being mad at Black parents. Fuck that shit. I felt like this was wrong. How can a Black kid be made a parent? Being mad at a parent made it seem like we were equal.

When I was growing up, I had a white friend that lived down the street from me. He used to always tell his mom that he was mad at her, and I would be scared, thinking, *Aw shit, it's about to go down. I can't do that shit at my house.*

Fuck the backpack - that's the real white boy shit! But anyway, it felt good to say it.

Auntie Pat: Hm. I honestly think that's a huge part of your issue. I could be wrong. But I think it is.

Me: My issue?

Auntie Pat: Not only have you been quiet all your life because you didn't feel like you could talk or go to your parents or anyone, for that matter, but you've been mad at your dad and that's what put the cap on the bottle. That's what sealed it.

Me: Really? Hmm.

Auntie Pat: I think it would do you some good to tell him. I think it would make you feel better.

Me: Hell nah. Tell my dad I'm mad? Are you fucking crazy? Shiiiid.

Auntie Pat: Hahaha. I think it would add to your healing. I think he needs to know, and I think it would do you some good. It may be healthy for you just to say it.

Heal? Damn I thought I was just fucked up. I thought I was going to therapy to get "unfucked up". I didn't know I needed to heal.

Me: Just say it?

Auntie Pat: Just say it. The objective is for you to release it. You don't know what he's going to say. Don't have any expectations. Just say it, and if a conversation happens, go from there but you need to just say it.

Me: And you think this will help me?

Auntie Pat: I do. But do it when you're ready. I think the sooner you say it, the sooner you can really begin releasing all those years of built up frustration. It seemed to have done you some good just admitting it to yourself a few minutes ago. Do you think it did?

Me: I do.

Auntie Pat: What do you think it will do for you if you said it to him?

Me: Well, first I'd be scared to say it. That nigga aint no joke. Hahaha. But I think it would make me feel better, a lot better. I wanna feel better. It would feel good to get it off my chest. I think you're right. I think it may free me up some.

Auntie Pat: How's you guys relationship? It seems like it's pretty good from the way you talk about him.

Me: Yeah, it's cool. We talk a lot. But in the back of my mind, I've always side eyed him, and I didn't know why. I've always felt like something kept me from being totally myself. Shit, I guess it was because I was mad. Damn, I didn't know that's what it was. But I'm so mad at him.

Auntie Pat: It could be some trust things there too. We'll talk about that in the next session. We're out of time.

Me: Damn! It was just getting good.

Auntie Pat: I know, I know. But the sooner you tell him, son, the better.

Me: Shiiid, I'm doing this shit today while it's on me.

Auntie Pat: That's a good idea. But do it when it's good for you. I'd be interested to see how the call goes. Take good notes, okay?

Me: Oh, I will, hahaha.

Auntie Pat: Hahaha, I'm sure. You'd be a great storyteller by the way. You have an interesting way of telling your stories.

Me: Hm. See you next time. Can I give you a hug?

Auntie Pat: Sure.

Me: Thanks Pat.

Auntie Pat: You're welcome, kid.

It was the first time we hugged. I'm not even sure if that's legal in the therapy world. But we hugged. We didn't make it a regular thing, but on that day, I think I needed it. It was actually better than her joining in with me to say, "Fuck you!"

I left happy and mad - happy I got this shit out but mad at my dad for leaving, and I'm bout to go tell his ass.

You ever been excited to tell someone you're mad at them? Well shit, I was.

CHAPTER 13
LOOKING FOR A FIGHT

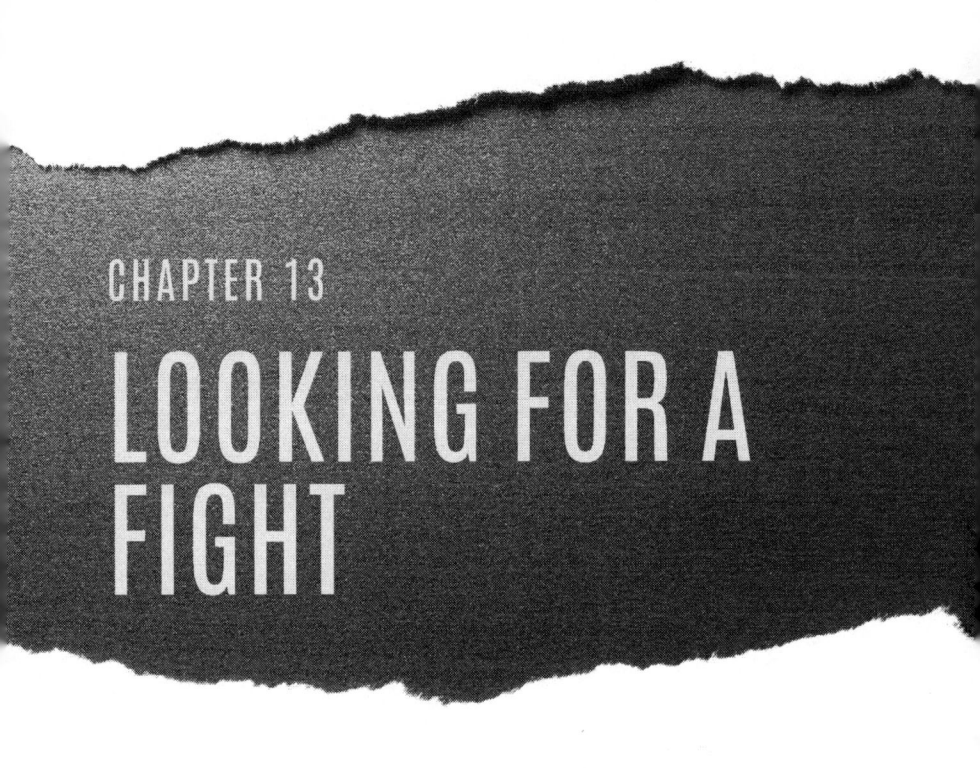

I left that therapy session ready to call my pops. I couldn't get home fast enough. I didn't want to call him in the car. I had to make important calls sitting in the house, not the car. I had to be sitting on the foot of my bed when I called him. That seemed to be my comfort zone.

The whole ride home, I'm practicing, "I'm mad at you. I'm mad at you. I'm mad at you."

Take a deep breath.

"I'm mad at you. I'm mad at you."

I got to get myself ready. Once he answers the phone, I gotta just say it. No small talk. Just say the shit. I just know we bout to argue. I ain't never argued with my pops. But I feel like today bout to be the day because he bout to hear the anger in my voice. And plus, I'm gone tell him I'm mad. Auntie Pat said don't have any expectations, but I'm expecting a fight.

I park the car and did that little walk-jog-walk inside the building. You know how you can be walking then you jog about four steps then yo ass walk again cuz you really ain't in shape to do a full run. That's the what the fuck I did- the walk-jog-walk.

I get on the elevator, press the 13. "I'm mad at you. I'm mad at you."

I walk in the crib and go straight to the foot of my bed. I sit down, take a deep breath and look at the phone. I know his number by heart. I only know about three numbers by heart - his number, my mama's number, and my own damn number. I don't even have to look for his name. I just dial the number.

It's ringing.

While it's ringing, let me tell you this right quick.

One thing I can say about my pops is that he always picks up the phone no matter what he's doing. He can be in a board meeting, "Hey Reg, I'm in a meeting, you ok? I'll call you right back." "Hey Reg, I'm in the middle of taking a shit, you okay? Let me wipe and I'll call you right back". "Hey Junior, I'm checking out, bout to get some chicken to put on the grill. You ok? I'll call you right back." When I say this man picks up his damn phone, he picks up his damn phone. And he always calls right back.

Pops: Hey Junior!

Me: I'm mad at you.

Pops: I'm in a meeting. Let me step out and call you right back.

He calls back in all of eight seconds. But it gives me time to stand up. I couldn't do this shit sitting like I thought I could. It's bout to go down.

The phone rings, and I answer.

Pops: Hey Reg. You said you were mad at me?

Me: Yeah man, I'm mad at you.

My dukes are up.

Pops: What did I do?

Me: You left me, man. And I'm mad at you.

Pops: Left you when?

Me: When you and mama got divorced. You went back to school and you left me.

He took a breath.

Pops: You know what, Reg? You right, I did leave you. But we talked about me leaving.

Putting my left fist down.

Me: Talked about it when?

Pops: Before I left.

Me: I don't remember that.

Pops: It's okay. You probably blocked it out. But me and your mom sat you down and talked to you about me leaving after your last surgery.

Aww hell, this nigga ain't tryna fight.

Me: I don't remember that.

Pops. It's okay, I get it. But me and your mama talked to you then. I sat you down and talked to you by myself and told you I was leaving. I told you I was going back to school. I told I wouldn't leave until you were done with all of your surgeries. I wanted to make sure you were okay first. You don't remember that?

I don't remember none of this shit. Damn, did I really block this shit out?

Me: No sir.

Pops: When you stopped having the surgeries, we asked you over and over were you sure and you said you were. I sat you down again by myself to make sure. And you don't remember that? Bless your heart. Damn.

Me: No sir.

Pops: I told you that once I felt like you were good and you were done with surgeries I was going to leave. You said you were good. So I left.

I don't remember none of that sitting down talking shit. All I remember is he left. That's all I remember.

Me: Man, I don't remember none of that. I just remember you left.

Pops: I get it. Do you wanna know why I left?

Me: Yeah, sure.

Pops: Well, you were getting ready to go to high school. You may not remember, but I was a junior high school principal, and I was coaching, making $36,000 a year. That may have seemed like a lot of money, but after paying all my bills, giving your mama child support and then giving you extra money too, I had $23 at the end of each check and teachers only got paid once a month. I was broke.

Me: Damn.

Pops: I couldn't save shit. You were about to turn 15, and I knew you wanted to go to college. Me and ya mama didn't have no money saved up. You were smart, but a scholarship wasn't a guarantee. And I wanted you to be able to go anywhere you wanted to go and not worry about money. Not have to get loans, grants or none of that shit. I needed to make more money. And the only way it was going to happen was if I went back to school. You said you were okay. So I left.

Me: Damn.

Pops: Remember you had a full scholarship to Prairie View? And at the last minute, you decided to go to Jackson State, and you hadn't even applied. They only had a little money left so you only got half a ride. But I said, don't worry. I got it.

Me: Damn.

Pops: Whenever you needed money for books. Room and board. Whatever it was. You asked me if you could get a job so you could have some spending money. What did I tell you?

Me: You said 'Don't get no damn job. You need to focus on yo grades. I got it.'

Pops: When you went to the University of Minnesota at the last minute and only got half a ride again, you said you wanted to get a student loan. I said, 'Nigga, don't you get no loan. I got it. And yo ass still went got a loan so you could hang out and buy clothes 'n shit. Crazy ass!'

Me: Hahaha! Damn. Yeah, I'm still paying on that shit.

Pops: That's why I left. I wanted to make sure you were good.

Me: Damn.

Pops: You think I would have just left you, man? C'mon bro.

Me: Yeah, I did at the time.

Pops: I understand why you think I just left you cuz you blocked it out. But I wouldn't just leave you, man.

Me: I know. My bad, man.

Pops: It's all good. You okay?

This time when he asked if I was okay, I was *really* okay because I didn't hold shit in.

Me: Yeah, man. I'm good. Love you, Dad.

Pops: Love you too, bro. Let me get back in this meeting and get these crazy mufuckas in line. Talk to you later.

I appreciated his rationale, but for some reason, it still didn't quite sit with me. I detected a hint of bullshit.

I hung up looking at the phone like, *What Tha Fuck! He shut my ass all the way up.* But it still didn't quite sit right with me. But I guess it made sense. Even though Auntie Pat told me not to have any expectations, I had some. I was expecting an argument. I was expecting some push back. Again, telling a Black parent you're mad at them can be some scary shit. I was expecting, "Mufucka I don't give a damn why you mad! You better get off my phone with that bullshit." I probably would have just responded, "Dang, my bad.", and that would have been the end of that.

Plus, when you call a mufucka while you're mad, you're kinda expecting a fight because you wanna fight. But this mufucka owned it, explained why, and didn't put up a fight. That was a waste of frustration, shit! Damn, I had blocked out an entire conversation that he and my mom had with me, an entire moment about that shit. Damn, he did not meet my expectations.

A day later, I was in a Waffle House parking lot, sitting on the phone with my boy Leon. He and his wife had just gone through a divorce and he said, "Man, I'm going to have to get up out of Little Rock, so I can make some more money. I can't make that much money here. My son bout to turn 15, and I need to start preparing for his college. I ain't tryna have that dude out here with these loans 'n shit."

I literally just sat there and said to myself, *Well I'll be damned. So preparing for your kids' future is some real shit.* I don't have kids, so the shit is foreign to me. That's a frame of mind I'm not familiar with at all. So just maybe he wasn't bullshitting. SMH. Funny how sometimes we gotta hear shit from somewhere else for it to be valid. Oh well, we are talking bout 30 plus years. I needed a second opinion, lol. My boy had no idea how that brief discussion about his situation provided validation, truth, comfort and answers to the shit I was dealing with.

However, my pops still left tho. Having him stay would have meant more. But I'm not a parent, so some predicaments and decisions I just don't get. If he had stayed, I probably would have had to stay at home and go to the Yard, which I wasn't having. I mean I love the Yard. But I needed to get out the Bluff. Too much had happened there. But I guess it all makes sense.

I wrote all this shit down in my journal. It actually felt good to write this shit. So he really didn't leave me. He just left. He left to prepare a better life for me. Ain't that some shit? And he was right, I never needed for anything money wise. If I ever did, he would wire or transfer that shit within minutes no matter the amount.

He gave up being there with me during my last years of high school, so I could have a better adult life.

Hell, I'm glad that nigga left, hahaha!

Myyy Nigga!

Auntie Pat may have been on to something. She just might know what the fuck she's doing. The next session is going to be awesome. She's going to be happy. Well, at least I'm happy.

THE AFTERTHOUGHT
CHOKE THAT LIL NIGGA

After we hung up, I kinda wished I would have brought up The Yard incident. I wish I would have told him that he could have at least protected me a little more by asking who called me that shit. I wish he would have went and choked that little nigga out or at least had a talk with his parents. Maybe it wasn't important at the time. Maybe his main concern was just making sure I was okay. Who knows? But I'm not going to bring it up anytime soon, maybe never. Hell, just letting him know I was mad was enough release to give me the closure I needed.

I also realized that this is why I had trust issues and was able to just abandon any type of relationship without notice - hell if my favorite dude could leave without telling me, I knew yo ass could too. So I didn't trust people to stay, nor did I give a fuck about leaving. But that's not the reality of why he left. Damn, this was some more shit I gotta work on - giving mufuckas a heads up before I leave. Do better Reggie.

CHAPTER 14
SMILING IN AND OUT

When I went back to therapy, I walked into the building with a big ass smile on my face as usual. I spoke to every damn body. The building didn't have a ton of energy. It was pretty quiet and peaceful. It was probably full of folks going to or coming out of therapy so people were probably processing or just getting their minds right. So, I can only imagine what folks were thinking, *Who's the happy nigga that comes in here every few days with a backpack and a piece of candy? Does anybody know the happy nigga?*

I had my shit ready to share. Hell, a few days before, I had a "Come to Jesus" talk with my pops. That really did a lot for me. I'm sure it probably did a lot for him as well. Therapy was the shit. I was actually healing. First, it was a place to unload and put my trash on the curb. Now, I was starting to find new pieces to put in that new space of mine. I wasn't even mad about it.

As usual, Auntie Pat was in her regular spot. She offered coffee, and, again, I took it. I needed to be sipping when we talked about this shit. She noticed the excitement on my face and the pep in my step, "Seems like somebody is having a good day." I said "You damn right." She chuckled and said, "Go ahead, and I'll be in in a second."

A few minutes later, she walked in with her notepad and coffee. She had the glasses on top of her head today. I think Auntie Pat was puttin a lil drank in her coffee. She was hearing about mufuckas' problems all day. She prolly needed to calm her own damn nerves. Just a random thought.

I pulled my notebook out. I didn't even read the shit. I just started talking.

Me: Well, I talked to my pops a couple days ago.
Auntie Pat: Well, walk me through it.
Me: I called him. Told him I was mad.
Auntie Pat: Okay! Okay! Did you have any expectations?
Me: I expected him to go off, but he didn't.
She smiled.
Auntie Pat: Okay great! Keep talking.
Me: He asked why I was mad. I told him because he left me.
Auntie Pat: Okay.
Me: Tha mufucka agreed that he left. He owned that shit. He said he understood why I would be mad.

Auntie Pat: So he understood and validated your feelings. Okay. What else?

Me: He said he and my mama talked to me about it. He said they told me he was leaving and I was okay with it. Then he told me by himself to make sure. And I said I was good. He said I must have blocked it out.

Auntie Pat: I can definitely see that. It was traumatic to you. He's your best friend. It's something you didn't want to happen. Something you didn't want to remember. That's actually normal. What else?

Me: He told me he left so he could make more money, so he would be able to pay for my college, and I wouldn't have to get loans and shit.

Auntie Pat: What do you think of that?

Me: It makes sense.

Auntie Pat: Did he help you with college?

Me: He did. I didn't have to pay for shit. Well I got loans that he told me not to get, but you know what I mean.

Auntie Pat: How do you feel about his reasoning?

Me: I feel good about it. He didn't leave me hanging. I guess that's shit you think about as a parent.

She was smiling.

Auntie Pat: It is. Tell me your thoughts on the overall conversation and how it ended.

I began to tell her word for word and how I felt. I told her it ended on a great note. A happy ending. I even told her about the call with my boy in the Waffle House parking lot. She thought the timing of that call was interesting.

Auntie Pat: The way you talk about your dad and you guys' relationship, I felt that it was more to it than you knew. I felt like he had an explanation that you could live with. I honestly didn't think that he would leave you high and dry like you felt he did. But I didn't want to tell you that. I wanted you to find out and hear it for yourself. I wanted you to have that conversation and get some answers. I wanted you to be able to get that frustration out and communicate that yourself. It's really important that you at least express your feelings and not harbor them. So it was important for you to be honest with him. And it sounds like he was very gentle with you, which I also like. Sounds like you have a pretty cool dad."

Me: Yeah, he aight, haha.

She chuckled too.

I don't remember us talking about the talk with my pops too much after that during that session. I do recall us getting on a lighter topic and discussing my RV dreams and music. Again, music was our shit.

I had been going to therapy on a weekly basis for about eight months at this point. I told her I was no longer mad at him, and I felt like I could move on to some other shit. That was a major breakthrough. Being able to tell him that kind of gave me the okay to open up period. But it wasn't going to happen overnight. I mean, I'd been quiet and not communicating for 30 damn years. The shit wasn't gone end just like that for me. For somebody else maybe, but not for me. I had to unlearn not communicating. I had to unlearn not expressing myself and thinking that crying was a sign of weakness - I had to unlearn all that shit.

Though my pops and I didn't get into the shit that I had to unlearn, just me telling him I was mad made me feel like opening up was okay. My healing had really ramped up. I was more conscious of it, but it was going to take some more work, and I had to be intentional. Oh trust me, I fell back into my old habits quite a bit, but I was aware of it, and I did my best to snap back into my new way of communicating and being. My reprogramming was happening.

Man, I loved expressing myself and was really getting into this healing thing so much so that I wanted to make sure I didn't miss shit. So I asked Auntie Pat if my ex-wife LaShonda could come to a session to give her side of things. I mean, just in case I blocked some shit out since apparently that was a thing for me, and Auntie Pat agreed.

LaShonda came to a couple sessions, and all that did was introduce more shit for me to work on, which was cool. I was all in at that point. I had leaned all the way into this healing and growing shit. Shiiid, I couldn't be stopped. I was glad LaShonda came because it helped with my healing process. Again, you'll get more of the marriage shit in another book. This book ain't bout that.

Even though we were dealing with some painful shit, it was still fun for me because I saw it working in my life. I saw a change in me - a positive change. Watching myself grow and heal was hella cool.

MUF*CKA

I was loving it. Auntie Pat was loving it. Not only did I walk in the building smiling, but now I walked out the mufucka smiling too.

CHAPTER 15
YOU GOT IT FROM HERE

Auntie Pat and I had been putting in work for almost 18 months. I was still getting in and out of the car the same way - smiling. I was still walking in and out of the building the same way - smiling. I would still go home the same way - smiling. Then I would journal. It was routine.

The last few sessions were wonderful and light-hearted. We laughed and talked about day to day shit and my RV trip and some of the places I would go.

She asked me what I wanted to do with my life. I told her how all I ever wanted to do was travel the world, be myself and inspire others to be themselves.

Auntie Pat: Well, I think you should do just that. I think you'd be awesome at that. People would love you.

Me: Really?!!

Auntie Pat: Yep, you're a special person. I'm not sure I've ever met anyone like you. As a matter of fact, I know I haven't.

Me: Wow! Thanks, that means a lot.

Auntie Pat: You just had some healing to do. I think you did that. Don't you? There's still more, but I think you understand the process. I think your parents did an awesome job with you. I think you should tell them that too.

Me: One day I will.

Auntie Pat: If you can, make it soon. This session is on me.

Me: Really!!! Thanks cuz yo ass ain't cheap.

Auntie Pat: Hahaha, and your sense of humor is everything. Hahaha.

Me: I mean, you know, haha.

Auntie Pat: I would love to keep taking your money, but I don't wanna take it anymore.

Me: So, the rest of the sessions are free?

Auntie Pat: Yeah, actually I think this should be your last session.

Wait, did she just break up with me?

Me: WHAT!!!??? WHY??!!!

She pushed up her black rimmed glasses on her face.

Auntie Pat: Well because I think you're good to go. I think you have the tools to move on. I think you've purged and got out a lot of the shit you needed to get out to move forward and be a greater guy than you were before. I just think you had to get that anger out and you did that. I think I've done all that I can with you. I think you just need to accept yourself - your scars, your hand, and all that. And that you can do on your own, in your own time. But it's going to happen. I feel like we've made room for it to happen for you now.

I was tearing up. Was I crying because I was going to miss the shit out of her or because I was happy I was growing and healing? I think it was both.

Me: Really!?

Auntie Pat: Yep! I do. You have been amazing to work with. I'm so proud of you. I think once you see yourself, you're going to give the world hell. I'm actually gonna miss you. But I can't keep taking your money. Go be greater, okay.

She was tearing up.

Me: Yes ma'am! Can we hug?

Auntie Pat: Sure we can.

Me: Well, c'mon bring that shit in.

We laughed and hugged.

Auntie Pat: Let's go! I wanna show you something.

Me: Where the hell we going? Haha.

She got up and headed out the office. I followed. As we passed the coffee maker, I couldn't help but to get a little sad because I thought, *This is probably the last time I'll ever see this coffee maker or her standing next to it wearing her little black rimmed glasses.*

We headed to the elevator full of laughter. I was sure people were thinking, *Who's the old white lady and the young nigga laughing and smiling?*

We walked outside. She pointed to a little grayish-blue sedan and pointed to the passenger side.

Auntie Pat: Door's unlocked, get in.

I looked in the passenger seat, and it was full of snacks and a bottle of water. She had peanut butter cups, chocolate chip cookies and some chips.

Me: Get the fuck outta here! You remembered!!

She burst into laughter. I got in and put all the snacks in my lap and started opening shit and smacking. Auntie Pat started fucking with the radio.

Auntie Pat: Remember me telling you bout the band I was in in high school?

Me: Hell yeah!

Auntie Pat: Well, I found an old tape. I wanted you to hear me rock out on the guitar, haha.

Me: Awww shit! Not rock out. I gotta hear this shit. Let me hear it got dammit.

She took her black rimmed glasses off and put on some shades. I fell out laughing. She turnt that shit up to the highest volume and sang her ass off. It was actually pretty decent.

We sat in the car, ate snacks and sang for at least 30 minutes. It was a good ass time. Me and Auntie Pat.

She looked at her watch...

Auntie Pat: Well I got another client coming in in a few minutes. This has been a lot of fun. I'm going to miss you kid.

Me: I'm going to miss you too and thanks.

Auntie Pat: Anytime. You better take that RV trip.

Me: I will. Don't you worry bout that.

She put her black rimmed glasses back on and placed the shades back in the visor. We got out of the car. I walked around it and gave her one more hug. She pushed her glasses up on her nose.

I put the rest of my snacks in my backpack.

She walked into the building.

And I walked to my car with a smile on my face and tears in my eyes.

Therapy was a success. I had breakthroughs and endearing moments with both parents. I wasn't mad anymore. I was communicating better. I was healing daily. I wasn't done with the work, but I was off to a great start. It was time to go and accept myself - whatever the hell that looks like.

Thanks Auntie Pat! You're the best!

CHAPTER 16
AHA MOMENT

I've been hurt. I've gone thru shit and I've conquered a lot of it. I've healed from a large portion of it. Honestly, therapy and what came out of it was only the first phase of my healing. The shit is ongoing, and I still got more to do, according to Auntie Pat. She said I still gotta accept myself and that'll eventually happen. And I was just waiting on that moment.

But let me tell you mufuckas something, after going to therapy for almost two years on the regular and realizing I had been quiet for over thirty years, there's not a damn thing I won't say. I'd been shut up all that time. I don't give a fuck about how somebody reacts to some shit I say. I say what I want when I want. I cuss and talk shit in business meetings, I cuss on church parking lots and I ain't turning the got damn music down either. I have a voice and mufuckas are about to hear it. If you cringe, then that's on you. Now, I guess you get why I named this book *Mufucka*. Exactly, cuz the shit liberates me. I feel free. It's the word that freed me from my pain. I feel like Reggie when I say that shit. The day after therapy, I think my usage of the word *mufucka* increased by 200%.

I bet y'all thought it was gone be some ole profound shit, didn't you? I bet y'all thought it was going to come at the end of the book then I was gone drop the mic, didn't you, lol? I rarely give you what you expect when you expect it. That aint my way. I'm Hathorn, baby. I'm not THAT predictable. lol.

So anyway, the world hadn't seen or heard the real me because hell, I'd been quiet. Shit, I hadn't seen the real me. I had to learn who this dude was. This liberated dude. This free dude. Who was he? I needed to learn who he was for myself.

But in the meantime, I was going to go tell the world bout this new person I was and talk some shit. Because booyyy did I have some shit to say.

What better place to talk some shit than the stage. What stage? The comedy stage.

It was September of 2015 when I started looking up comedy classes. Because if I was going to do this, I wanted to know what the fuck I was doing and be good at it. I found a six month course, and I enrolled in that shit immediately.

I got to class and there were about 20 folks in there. There was all kinda people - old people, young people, white folks, latinos, Blacks, teachers, bankers, unemployed mufuckas, cashiers. Everybody was enrolled to learn how to be funny or write a good joke. I enrolled because I was told comedy was a good way to let off some steam and a creative way to get your story out. That's why I was there. I wasn't trying to be funny. I just wanted to talk some shit and get my story out.

The first night, we met our teacher, Dave. He was a short, middle aged white dude with a blonde comb over, wearing raggedy jeans with run down shoes. He talked about the history of comedy, what to expect from the class, and his teaching style. I was sitting there like *Shit, you look funny yo damn self.* He coulda just said, "Look at me. I'm comedy.", and we all could have just got up and walked the fuck out after that.

He piqued my interest when he said we were required to journal our day every day, and if we hit an "aha moment" that's the shit we were to find something funny to expound on. I'm like hell, *I've been writing every day for the last two years. This ain't gone be shit.* I just had to write with a different purpose. This is bout to be interesting. I liked it because I still got to journal. I still got to write about my day.

So, the direction of my journaling had changed. But it was still journaling, and, in my own way, I was still healing and cleansing just in a different way. I guess it was cool.

Just like Auntie Pat, Dave wanted us to read shit from our journals out loud to the class. But, I wasn't just reading to Auntie Pat anymore. I was reading to other mufuckas, telling them about my day and hearing about theirs. Hm. That was different. But Dave listened with a different ear. He was listening for the aha moment - the joke. The class was also listening for the humor. And once we found the aha moment, just like Auntie Pat in therapy, Dave wanted us to explore that shit and dig deeper. Hm, this is interesting.

Here's the thing tho, if it wasn't funny, they didn't think it was good. That's the part I didn't like. I didn't like feeling like I had to be funny. I just wanted to talk shit, honestly. Being funny was the least of my concerns. I just wanted to be honest and genuine. If the shit ended up funny, cool. If it wasn't funny, you were at least going to get honest.

One night, he invited the class to see him perform at a comedy club in Addison, TX. He said he was given 15 minutes. That's a pretty decent set. I couldn't wait to see him. The entire class was excited. Everybody was exchanging numbers and shit. We set it up, so we could sit together and see our comedy master at work. We wanted to see the dude that had been teaching us over the last month or so do the shit he was teaching us how to do.

About 16 of us showed up. We all sat together at about five tables we pushed together. Before Dave came out, we were laughing and tossing back drinks and shit. Mufuckas were practicing jokes amongst each other. A table full of corny mufuckas trying to be funny is a nightmare. I was sitting there like, *Oh my God would these mufuckas let it go!*

Then, the emcee came out and introduced our comedy master. We gave this mufucka a standing ovation before he said one word. We were all like, *Dave bout to kill it.*

Some of my classmates were laughing their asses off. They were taking shots and shit just having a good ass time, saying shit like, "Dave is awesome, hahaha!" But, I was like, *These mufuckas just happy to be out the house.* They were just like the mufuckas dancing to "Da Butt."

After he was about seven minutes in, I stood up, took the last swig of my drink, set the glass back on the table, touched the shoulder of the guy sitting next to me, and said "Y'all take care." He said, "See you in class tomorrow Reggie." I said, "Sure." and walked out.

I never saw Dave or any of my classmates ever again after that night.

I still continued to use his and Auntie Pat's journaling methods. I was writing and reflecting my ass off. It was crazy how random moments in my life were just popping up. Some of the moments made me laugh my ass off, some put me in deep thought and others made me cry. One morning after some intense ass journaling, I woke up and thought about a conversation I had with a close friend, Yolanda, that I had totally forgot about. Honestly, I'm not sure if I forgot about it or I blocked it out - you know how I do shit - I'm a "blocker outer". The conversation she and I had was worth sharing with the world; I didn't even think about it. I just went straight to my Facebook page and started writing a recap of the moment we had.

I just want you to see it for yourself -

MUF*CKA

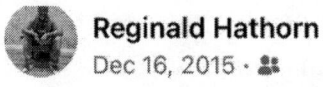

Reginald Hathorn
Dec 16, 2015

I STOPPED HIDING: About 6 years ago I was talking to my close friend, Yolanda. We were shooting the shit like normal you know just the typical check in that close friends do. We talked about the normal stuff: marriage, work, college memories, and the life happenings of mutual friends. But then Yolanda took the conversation to another level.

She asked me a question that changed my life.

Yolanda: "Hey man, I was looking at the picture we took at homecoming and some other pictures on your Facebook page."

Me: Oook

Yolanda: So why do you always hide when you take pictures?

Me: (playing stupid but shocked) What do you mean?

Yolanda: You know exactly what I mean. Why do you always hide your face? I've noticed you always stand behind people to hide your scar. Why?

Me: No I don't. Do I? I didn't know I did that. (knowing damn well that I did)

Yolanda: Yeah you do. I've noticed that on all your pictures. Stop doing that. You don't have to do that.

Me: Really? Let me go look.

Yolanda: Ok. Let's look at a few.

We both went to my Facebook Photo Gallery and scrolled through my pictures. She began to point out several pictures in which I was hiding.

Yolanda: See... See... See. All of them. You're hiding.

Me: Damn I do. I didn't know I did that. I wonder why I do that.

Yolanda: You know why you do it and it ain't cool. So stop, ok.

Me: I'll do my best.

Yolanda: No. Stop.

Man, I remember the day she told me to stop hiding. It was crazy. I couldn't believe she actually said that shit to me. No one had ever put the shit in my face like that. It threw me off. I actually didn't know how to take it. I didn't know if I should be mad about it or glad that I had someone in my life that loved me enough to call me out and challenge me to be myself. It took me a minute to process that shit.

Damn that post still moves me. It was a defining moment for me. It took a lot for me to write that post. I wrote it with tears in my eyes and a smile on my face. I felt like sharing it would help me get it out of my system and show her appreciation. People's reactions to it were really encouraging, uplifting and heartfelt. I had no idea it would help people, but the comments showed otherwise.

The post was up for about 15 minutes and Yolanda called me crying. Hell, hearing her cry made me cry all over again. This was the first time we had talked since she told me to stop hiding. I thanked her and told her how much I appreciated her for putting it in my face because it forced me to deal with not hiding my scars.

She said, "Dude, I'm so glad you posted that because I thought you were mad at me because you didn't call me for bout three years after that. I thought I'd lost a friend. I just wanted you to stop doing that shit."

I was like, "Yeah I know, my bad. I had to process that shit. You put it in my face. No one had ever done that. Then life took over and I never got back around to calling you. But nah, you didn't lose a friend. If anything, it made me love you more as a friend."

We both said I love you to each other, and we both changed our profile pics to the one of me hiding behind her. It was a moment we both needed in our own way.

It was cool to speak my truth and tell part of my story on social media.

Hiding behind Yolanda at Jackson State homecoming 2009

On February 5th of 2016, just a few months after I left Dave's ass on stage and stopped hiding behind folks, I posted my first video on social media. It was of me apologizing to a little four year old kid named Trayvion - the son of a girl I dated in my early 20s. I treated him differently because he wasn't the cutest little kid. But he had the cutest shoes. I wouldn't do shit with Trayvion because he wasn't that cute. I wouldn't pick him up from daycare. If he cried, I just looked at his ass. I wouldn't even hold his hand in Target. I just let Trayvion run wild in the store. He would always find me tho. He was really good with directions.

People were confused. They didn't know if I made this shit up or not. I was like, *Umm this shit is true.* I needed the adult Trayvion to know I was wrong and I was sorry.

Some people ripped me to shreds. I mean their asses let me have it.

"How yo ugly ass gone call a kid ugly?"

"Fuck you, what the fuck is going on with yo face?"

"You the last one to call somebody ugly."

"Mufucka, look at your nose."

You name it; I heard it. It was nothing I hadn't heard before. I must admit some of it stung a little because it was coming from mufuckas all over the world.

But then some laughed their asses off. Some of them even commented, "Even if the shit is true, it's still funny." A handful of people confessed that they'd treated a "kid with cute shoes" different before too, and it was bold to see somebody admit that shit on social media.

Before I posted the video, I had 800 followers - my friends and family. The video got over 10,000 views. After it finished circulating, I had over 2,000 followers.

I was like, *What the fuck! My shit more than doubled in four days. Hmm, you mean mufuckas like hearing truthful shit, shit that's honest? Well, I got something for their asses.*

So my career in talking honest shit on social media began and I got my friend back.

CHAPTER 17
YOU'RE NOT FUNNY

You can't stop me now. I got a lot of shit I wanna say. There's a lot of shit that I've been wanting to talk about. I am comfortable talking about shit now because I'd been quiet for over thirty years. You want content - I got content.

I am doing video after video, pushing them shits out every day. I am talking about everyday shit that I am going through or had been through and random shit that I'm thinking. I am even giving my opinion on shit trending topics and folks are sharing and commenting on my shit. My following is growing like crazy. I'm like, *This shit is easy.*

In my first 30 days, I had a video to go viral and hit over two million views. By mid March, I had over 15,000 followers, and all I was doing was talking shit.

One day I was journaling, and it hit me, *I need to take this shit serious. Get a comedy mentor. I need somebody that has experience in this shit. Somebody that you have actually seen before, not like Dave's whack ass. Somebody that can teach me something. Somebody that can actually help me grow.*

And as usual, I read that shit out loud to myself. Auntie Pat taught me that, haha.

I knew exactly who I was going to contact. A few months ago, I had seen this comedian named Shuckey Duckey at a fundraiser. I remember him from being on TV in the 90's. He was known for saying "Shuckey Duckey Quack Quack". That was his schtick. I hated his comedy then. I thought his shit was goofy. But that night at this little fundraiser, his shit was hilarious. I couldn't stop laughing. I didn't even know he was still in the game. I was like, *Damn, he's gotten a lot better. I fucks with this dude. Anybody that has been in the game that long and is still going, I need that mufucka as a mentor.* Plus, he was local.

I knew exactly how to reach him. When I was teaching back in the day, his daughter CeCi used to hang out in my class all the time to laugh and talk shit. She was a great kid, and I liked her. She was always doing some silly shit. We were Facebook friends, so I hit her up and asked if her dad mentored aspiring comics and if he did, would he be my mentor.

She said she wasn't sure, but she'd get back to me.

A few weeks later on March 29, 2016, we had this text exchange.

Ceci: ...Give him a call. He knows you are calling him.

She included his phone number.

Me: "What's his real name?"

Ceci: Cecil or Shuckey.

Damn, this nigga's name is Cecil! Fuck it! I started jumping up and down. I was punching the air. I was like *Awww shit, I got this nigga's real phone number. I'm bout to learn me some shit.* I picked up my backpack to go somewhere and journal because I had to write this shit down. I couldn't write this in the house. This had to be at a coffee shop or a bar, anywhere but the house.

I dialed his number on the way out the door, and before I could lock it, he answered. I was nervous as fuck. I didn't think the mufucka would actually answer. You know stars be wanting you to leave them a message 'n shit. They be wanting to call you back on their time. They funny like that. But this mufucka answered.

Me: Hey Cecil, this is Reggie!

Cecil: I knew you would call. What you doing?

Damn, what is this nigga - my daddy or something?

He got straight to the point. My pops is like that. He gets straight to it.

Me: Uhhh, I'm bout to go just hangout, not sure yet.

Cecil: Come to the shop.

Damn, this nigga got straight pops vibes. He didn't give a fuck bout what I had to do.

Me: Shop? What shop? Where is it?

Cecil: The barbershop. It's on 8th and Corinth. It's called blah blah.

I can't remember the name of it right now, and I don't feel like calling this nigga to get the name of it. I'm too busy writing this chapter. It's not important. Just keep reading.

Me: Aww, I know where that is. It's about …

Mid sentence, this nigga hungs up. I was trying to say his shop is about five to ten minutes from me. It's right across the bridge from where I live. That's what I was trying to say, but this rude ass nigga...

I threw my backpack in the passenger seat, started the car, and turned up my boy Prince. I can't remember the song. I just knew it was Prince. *I'm just starting to realize that I play the hell out of some Prince.* And I drove across the bridge singing at the top of my lungs. The drive was only five minutes.

I pulled into the parking lot and there was a bunch of cars and work vans and shit in the parking lot. I'm like, *What tha fuck is going on?* He and about four or five other OGs were talking. Some were standing and some were sitting on the hood of a van. It was the true OG scene. It woulda been a cool shot if I had had a camera.

I walked up with my backpack over my right shoulder and said "Hey what's up, how y'all doing?"

They all spoke, but they looked at me like, *Who is this nigga with the backpack? That's some white boy shit.*

Cecil said, "Gone in the shop young man. I'll be there in a sec."

I walked in and just stood in one spot til he got there. I looked around at the posters and pics on the wall. It was a small shop. It felt like a shop just for the homies. Nothing extravagant.

I kept thinking, *What is he bout to teach me?*

He walked in. He was about 5'11 or 6 feet. He was dark brown, wearing glasses, jeans, a button down shirt and a baseball cap.

He came up to me and stuck his hand out to shake it.

Cecil: I'm Cecil.

I pulled my hand out of my pocket.

Me: I'm Reggie.

Then he sat in a barber chair. I stood about five or six feet from him.

Cecil: Nice to meet you. That's a raggedy ass hand you got there.

Damn, this nigga holds no punches. I had heard the shit before. But I appreciated him saying it to my face.

I chuckled.

Me: Yeah, it is.

Cecil: Oh, I know. It's raggedy as hell. Do you know why I said that to you?

Me: Kinda. But I'm not sure. Tell me.

Cecil: I said it because your hand is different. It's unfamiliar to people. When you're on stage, they are going to stare at you. They won't focus on you. They won't focus on what you're saying. They won't give a shit about what you have to say because your hand is going to draw attention.

I never took my journal out or I would have been writing this down. But I needed to be in this moment.

Me: Ok

Cecil: So, you're going to have to get their attention off your hand to your voice.

Me: Ahh...

This nigga is diving straight in. He didn't even ask how my day was. Kinda rude.

Cecil: The way to do that is to bring it up before they get a chance to. Go ahead and mention it. Bring attention to it. It helps take their guard down when you do it first. Everybody got some shit wrong with them but when you bring it up first, they get comfortable with you, and now they'll listen to what you have to say.

Me: Yes sir. Got it.

Cecil: But when you do it, make it funny. That takes the pressure off you and them. That releases the tension in the room. After that you can go ahead and talk and get into your set.

He told me some other shit about why he got into comedy and some personal shit. But that's his story to tell.

Me: Yes sir. I gotchu.

Cecil: You don't have to call me sir. I appreciate it, but I ain't that damn old.

Me: Hahaha, gotchu.

Cecil: Now what happened to your hand?

Me: I was burned in a house fire when I was one month old. And the doctors...

Cecil: Stop. Don't nobody wanna hear that shit on this stage. Remember, get the attention off your hand and make it funny. I'll tell you what happened.

*How is this mufucka gone tell me what happened to **my** hand?*

Me: What happened?

Cecil: Well, yo ass look like a backpack bomber. They sent you to do a job one day. They wanted you to blow up a small village. They packed yo bag with all types of explosives and right before you threw the bag, the mufucka blew up in yo hand.

Me: Hahaha. Good one.

He kept a straight face.

Cecil: Yeah, that was pretty good. Don't get on that stage with the sentimental shit. Remember get them off your hand and make it funny.

Me: I got it. Hahaha.

Cecil: I saw some of your videos. I don't think you're funny.

Me: Okay. But you know...

Cecil: Nah, don't explain yourself. It's not about me. Fuck me. It's about what YOU want to say. I just don't like deadpan. You're a deadpan comedian. You're just a straight faced comic. No emotion comic. That's fine. Whatever works for you and your audience. Have you had any training?

Me: Yeah, I took this one class from this guy.

Cecil: Dave?

Me: Yeah, you know him?

Cecil: Yeah, I know him. Okay, that explains it.

Yeah, it did because Dave was pretty much the only stand up comedy teacher in the area.

Me: Hahaha

Cecil: But son, I need you to be unapologetic about who you are. You don't have to explain yourself, not to me or anyone else. Okay.

Me: Okay.

Cecil: Love who you are. Learn who you are. Show them who you are. Embrace who you are. Laugh at who you are. Be comfortable with who you are. Be kind to who you are. Be honest about who you are. Be bold about who you are. It's okay to be who you are. No one needs to approve who you are, and accept who you are.

Damn. I was soaking all this in.

Me: Got it.

Cecil: Good. Now why did you get into comedy?

Me: Well first, I've been through a lot.

Cecil: Obviously.

Me: Hahaha! Good one.

Cecil: Hahaha! I'm pretty good, ain't I? Keep going.

Me: Honestly man, I just want to show people that no matter what you've been through you can still find a reason to laugh. I want to show people that you can just be yourself. And, it's okay to be yourself. When I do videos, I know people are talking shit about me. But I'm okay with it. I want to show people who are scared to show their face or be themselves that they can. I do videos to take the hit for the people who are scared to take the punches. I want them to get the courage to show their faces too. It's more than comedy for me.

Cecil: Damn. I like you. Most people come in and say they think they're funny and want to make people laugh. Those are the people I really don't want to work with. But you, I like that. I'll be more than happy to be your mentor.

Me: Thanks. How much are you going to charge me?

Cecil: Let's not even worry about that.

He got up from the chair and walked over to a poster on the wall advertising an upcoming comedy show he was hosting. He pointed to it.

Cecil: I got this show this weekend. It's $25. I don't care if you come to the show or not, but I want you to buy a ticket. We'll start there.

Me: Aw shit! I can do that.

Cecil: Cool. Well, see you tomorrow at the same time.

I was in his shop for a couple hours. He shared a bunch of other personal shit. But again, that's his story to tell.

MUF*CKA

We shook hands and I left out that barber shop with so much excitement. The OGs were gone by this time. When I got in the car, I threw my backpack in the passenger seat, sat there a second and smiled. I drove back across the bridge in total silence with a smile on my face. But my mind was all over the place. I was ready. I had somebody that was going to help me project my voice, and he was the perfect person.

Normally, I'm not a fan of barber shop conversations because they talk about a bunch of shit that I'm not interested in, but this one - I enjoyed this one.

Later that night, the girl I was dating at the time, Camera Girl came over. I called her Camera Girl because she was the camera operator for most of my videos in the beginning. She had no experience, by the way. But she was good. She accepted the nickname and wore it proudly. Anyway, I told her I had met Shuckey Duckey, and the excitement started all over again. She was like "Damn, that nigga a legend!", and I was like, "I know." I went to his Facebook page and the nigga had sent me a friendship request. Awww shit, I'm Facebook friends with a legend. I know a legend. A legend is my mentor. What a way to end the day and go to sleep.

Who knew there was a legend right across the bridge? And the mufucka was my mentor - GOT DAMN!!!

CHAPTER 18
A THOUSAND WORDS

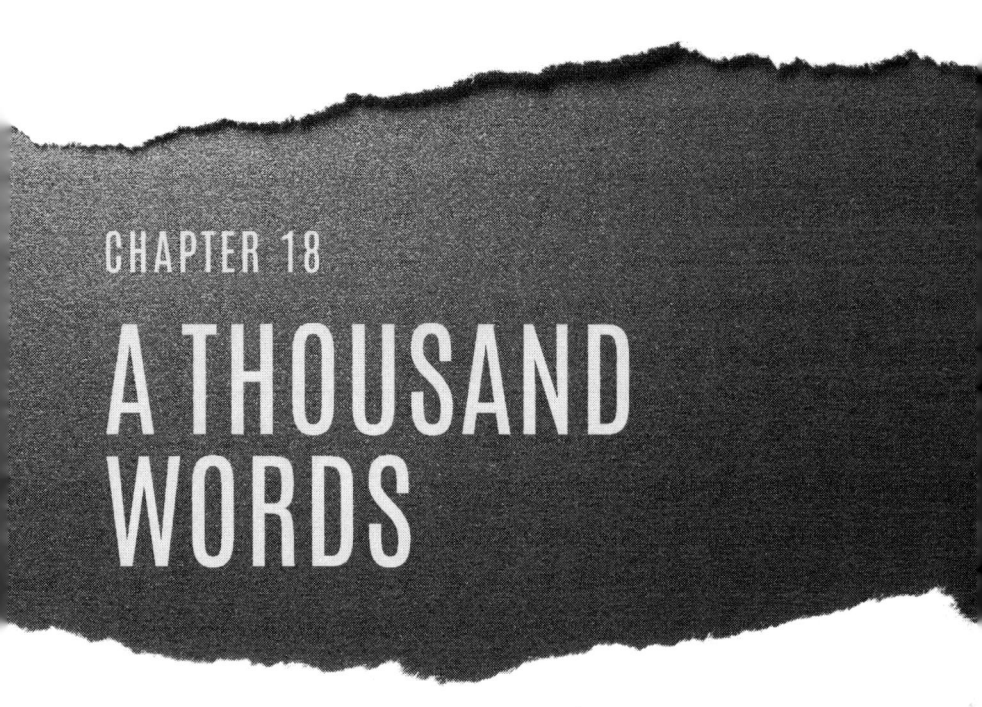

The next morning, I woke up in such a different space. Something felt different. I had an anxiousness that I couldn't explain.

I hopped out the bed with no shirt on and grabbed my phone. I woke up Camera Girl. She still had sleep in her eyes, but I didn't give a fuck. I handed her my phone.

Me: I want you to take a picture of me.

Camera Girl: Damn, let a sister wake up. How you gone pose?

I stood against the wall and put my right hand in front of my face, holding it with my left. I wanted my hand to be the main focus.

She took one shot, and without looking at it, she handed me the phone.

Camera Girl: What ya think?

Me: Damn. That's nice. I see you, Camera Girl.

I turned the phone around to her.

Camera Girl: Damn, that's a work of art. What you gone do wit it?

Me: I have no fucking idea. I just wanted to take a pic.

Camera Girl: Well, the shit is nice. It's actually pretty powerful. Damn! I still can't believe Shuckey Duckey your mentor tho. That's so cool.

Me: I know, right.

We got dressed and went on bout our regular day. She went to work, and I started delivering laundry.

The whole day I kept wondering about what Cecil was going to teach me later on. I was excited. Was he going to teach me some word play, timing, storytelling, how to work the crowd? What was I going to learn?

I picked up and delivered laundry all over Dallas and some of its suburbs. I went to Carrollton, Plano, Mesquite, Frisco - all over the city. I was leaving Frisco, heading south on the tollway exiting to get on Hwy 121 to head west. My phone was in the passenger seat. I picked it up to change the song, and it was on the picture that Camera Girl took that morning. That was weird. It's funny how sometimes you pick up your phone, and it'll be showing some shit that you weren't even looking for. I just looked at it. I pulled over on the shoulder of the freeway and just sat there for a sec. I looked at my hand. I stared at it. I had actually never seen a picture of it. I mean, of course, I had seen my hand but not in a picture. That was crazy. I just continued to sit there looking at all the details. The lines. The scars. The skin texture. The crooked bends in my fingers. The fingernails and how they all were different. It took me back to that day at the Yard when I noticed it was different for the first time.

Then I started thinking of all that shit Cecil said *"Love who you are, be honest about who you are, embrace who you are..."* - all that shit.

At that moment, still on the shoulder of a busy freeway, I started making a slideshow using the pic that Camera Girl had taken of me earlier that day. All of this was inspired by the shit that Cecil had said to me the day before.

When I finished, the changing position of the sun made me realize that I had been sitting on the side of a busy freeway for quite a while. I looked at the slideshow, and said "Damn, this cool." I was about to put the car in drive and something said to put some music on it. I was like okay. It was a no brainer. I went straight to "I Can Only Be Me". This was my song. It sums up my story. So duh. I went to my playlist, grabbed the song and added the audio. Voila! I had a fully produced slide show. It was some amateur shit, but it was cool enough for me. When I played the video, a damn tear rolled down my cheek, and I started singing the song.

You know how you get loud and sing harder on the part of the song that touches yo spirit the most? Man look, when the song asked if we would love the person we are when all the masks were off and there was no pretending - I got loud as hell right there. I was tired of not giving the real Reggie to the world. Shit, I was tired of not giving me the real Reggie. I wanted the covers to come off, so that part hit harder than it ever hit. I was singing with the 'ugly face'. When a mufucka sing with the 'ugly face' the song has just crossed the line and become a testimony - the shit is personal.

Then I heard God.

God: Bravo! Nice.

Me: Damn, I didn't even know you were listening.

God: Dude, I'm always listening. Post it, nigga. You got some followers. Share it.

Me: God, are you out yo mind? I ain't posting this. Gone somewhere with that bullshit, God.

He laughed.

God: Reg, post it. I got you.

Me: Man whatever. I'm not showing my hand.

God: Reg, pull ya hand out ya pocket and show it.

Me: No. Leave me alone. They ain't finna be laughin' at me.

God: Trust me. It's bigger than that. I promise you, I got you.

Me: Okay. But if they laugh at me God, we gone have a problem.

God: Hahaha, I got you son. Just do it.

Me: Aight Man, I trust you.

I went to my personal and my fan pages on Facebook. First, I changed my profile pic on each one to the pic of me holding my hand. If I was gone do it, I was going all the way in. If I was gone trust Him, I was gone push Him. I was going to give Him all of it. He didn't say do the profile pics, but to hell with it. Then I posted the video. The caption was "Be Who You Are."

I sat on the corner of the freeway exit and cried for a good 15 minutes straight. I had to get out the car and cry because it was too much for me to sit on. I walked around the car crying. I hit the hood of the car while I was crying. I screamed. And I cried some more.

I can only imagine what people passing by were thinking. I'm sure they were thinking something like *Who's the nigga on the corner of the tollway and 121 walking around his car screaming and crying?* Uuhh...That would be me.

I got back in the car and sat there for a sec. For the first time in over 30 years, I pulled my hand out my pocket. It hadn't been exposed that much. Maybe that explained the texture - the wrinkled yet smooth skin. It had been in the dark for so long, but it felt amazing to have it out of my pocket.

I was scared to go look at my page. I kept getting notifications and text messages, but I didn't read them. I cried some more. I just knew folks were laughing at me. I just knew it. I had missed calls, but I didn't return them.

God: Go 'head, look at your page.

Me: God I'm scared. I know they are laughing like they did the last time someone saw it.

God: Just look at it.

I opened my page. The comments were nothing like I thought. All I saw was shit like "amazing", "powerful", "sexy", "motivating", "inspiring", "OMG I needed this", "What happened?", "You're so strong", "I wish I had your strength". In short, I saw all good shit. And if somebody laughed, I didn't hear it.

My inbox was full of messages. People were telling me their stories, people wanted me to speak to their kids, people were showing me their scars, etc.

In less than an hour, the video had over 3,000 views. Wow. Just wow!

I started crying even more. I thought, *Damn just how many tears does a body hold?*

God smiled at me.

God: See nigga, I told you I had you. Now get back on the road and get those people their clean laundry, hahaha.

I pulled onto the freeway. I was smiling and crying.

Me: Myyyy nigga!!!!

God: Hahaha I love you, kid.

Me: Love you too, G!

I delivered everyone's laundry that day with a smile on my face and a tear in my eye.

I later pulled over and started responding to the messages. It was so cool. It felt good knowing that people didn't laugh at me showing my hand. They were inspired by it. I felt good knowing that something I'd covered up for so long was encouraging people. I might be on to something.

Damn near every time I visit Dallas, I go park in that exact spot on the tollway and 121 and I just sit there. I think about the conversation I had with God. I think about the conversation I had with myself. I think about how the flood gates had been opened. It's such a peaceful space for me. I got a fresh start right there on the shoulder of the freeway - well, ain't that some shit.

March 30th is a day I'll never forget.

CHAPTER 19
CROSSING THE BRIDGE

I got home, cried, smiled and responded to people's messages until about 5:45. Then, it was time to go across the bridge and see my guy Cecil.

I threw my backpack in the passenger seat. I drove across the bridge in total silence. I was trying to get my mind right for that day's lessons. I'm like shit, *If it's just half the message of yesterday's, it's going to be amazing.*

I pulled up in the parking lot. There weren't as many cars today. No OGs sitting on hoods or standing around talking shit.

I grabbed my backpack and headed inside.

Cecil was sitting in the same chair he was sitting in the day before. He was just chilling.

We shook hands, and he chuckled.

Cecil: You and this damn backpack.

I chuckled.

Cecil: How you doing today?

Me: I'm good bro. How you doing?

Cecil: I'm good bro. I saw your video.

He shifted in his seat. He leaned forward, put his elbows on his knees, and clasped his fingers.

Me: Oh cool. You saw it.

Cecil: Yeah. I liked it. I liked it a lot.

Me: Cool.

Cecil: You don't need me to be your mentor.

Me: What?!

I know he said he didn't think I was funny but damn. He just gone drop my ass off like that.

Cecil: You don't need me. You have everything you need.

Me: I don't get it.

Cecil: Your video. You showing your hand. Have you ever done that before?

Me: No, I haven't.

Cecil: That's what I thought. So, there you go. That's all you needed to do. You're good. It's nothing else I can do for you.

Me: So that's all I needed? No more meetings?

Cecil: Yep, that's it. No more meetings.

Me: Damn. That was fast.

He just shrugged his shoulders and smiled.

Me: Sooo, what do I do from here?

Cecil: Just go be yourself.

Me: Just go be myself. Well oookay. I guess that's what I'll do. So just go be Reggie. I can do that.

Cecil: Good. Go do it.

Me: Welp, I guess it was nice meeting you. And hey, thanks bro. I appreciate it.

We shook hands.

Cecil: Don't worry bout it. Nice meeting you too, bro.

I straightened my backpack on my shoulders and took a step towards the door.

Cecil: Say, give my got damn $25 for that ticket. Nigga you ain't gone get outta here without giving me my money.

Me: Hahahaha

I handed him the $25

Cecil: Nigga think he slick hahaha.

He patted me on the shoulder, and I walked out.

I stood in the parking lot for a few minutes before I got in the car. Damn, I guess I just needed to accept myself and pull my hand out my pocket. Hm - imagine that. Why didn't he just say that, hahaha?

I started smiling and dancing by myself in the parking lot where the OGs had stood the day before. I thought about that little eight year old boy in his bedroom playing dress up wanting to be someone else. I stretched my arms and raised them to the air and said,

"Ladies and gentlemen, coming to the stage - REEGGIEEEE HAAATHOOORRN."

The Beginning

Embrace

Who You Are

No One Needs to Validate Who You Are

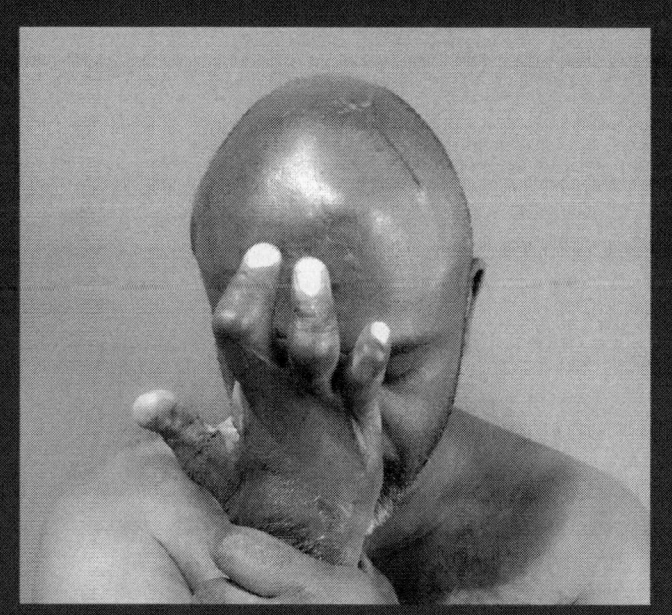

It's Okay To Be Who You Are

Be Honest About Who You Are

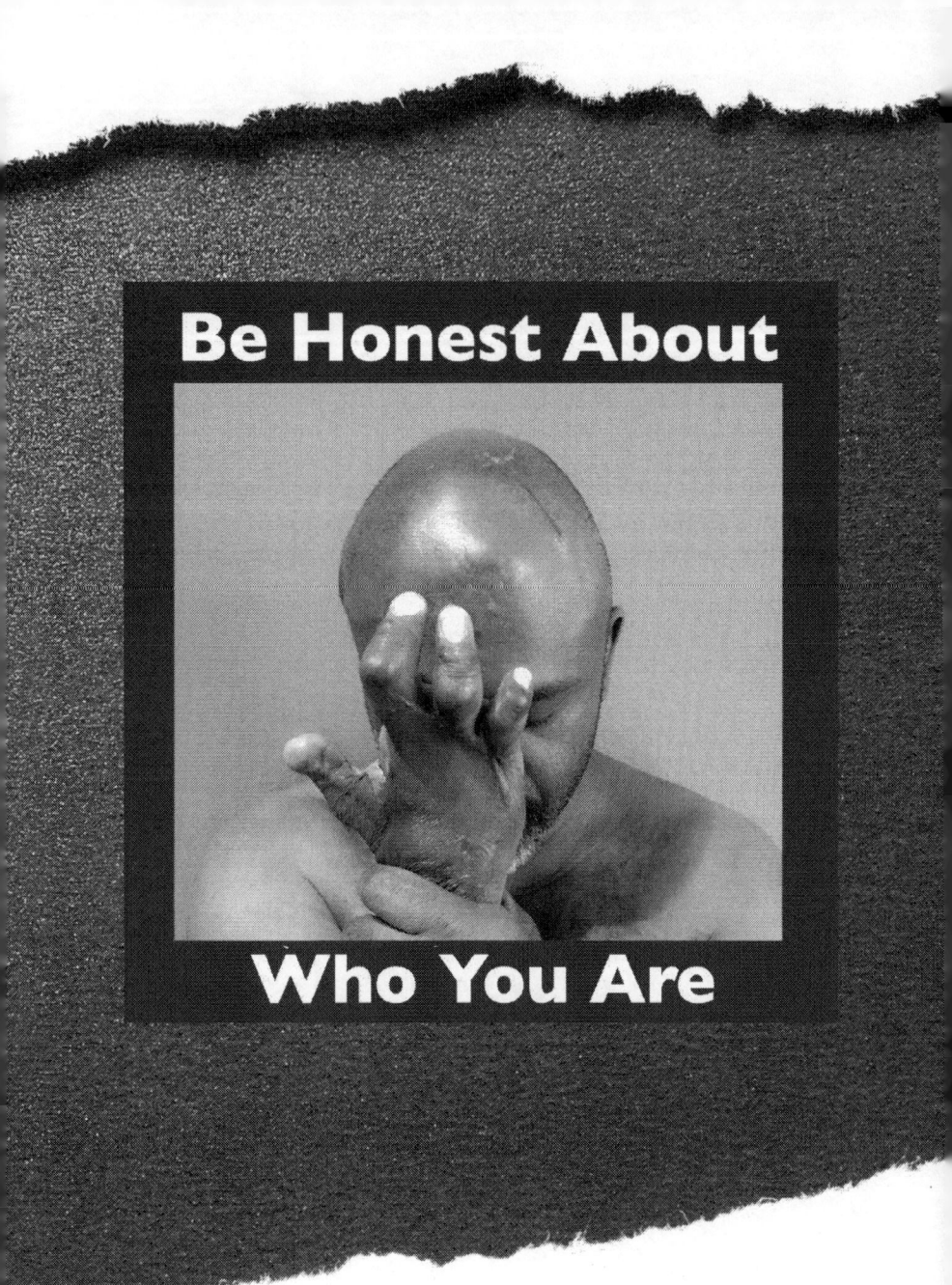

Be NonApologetic About Who You Are

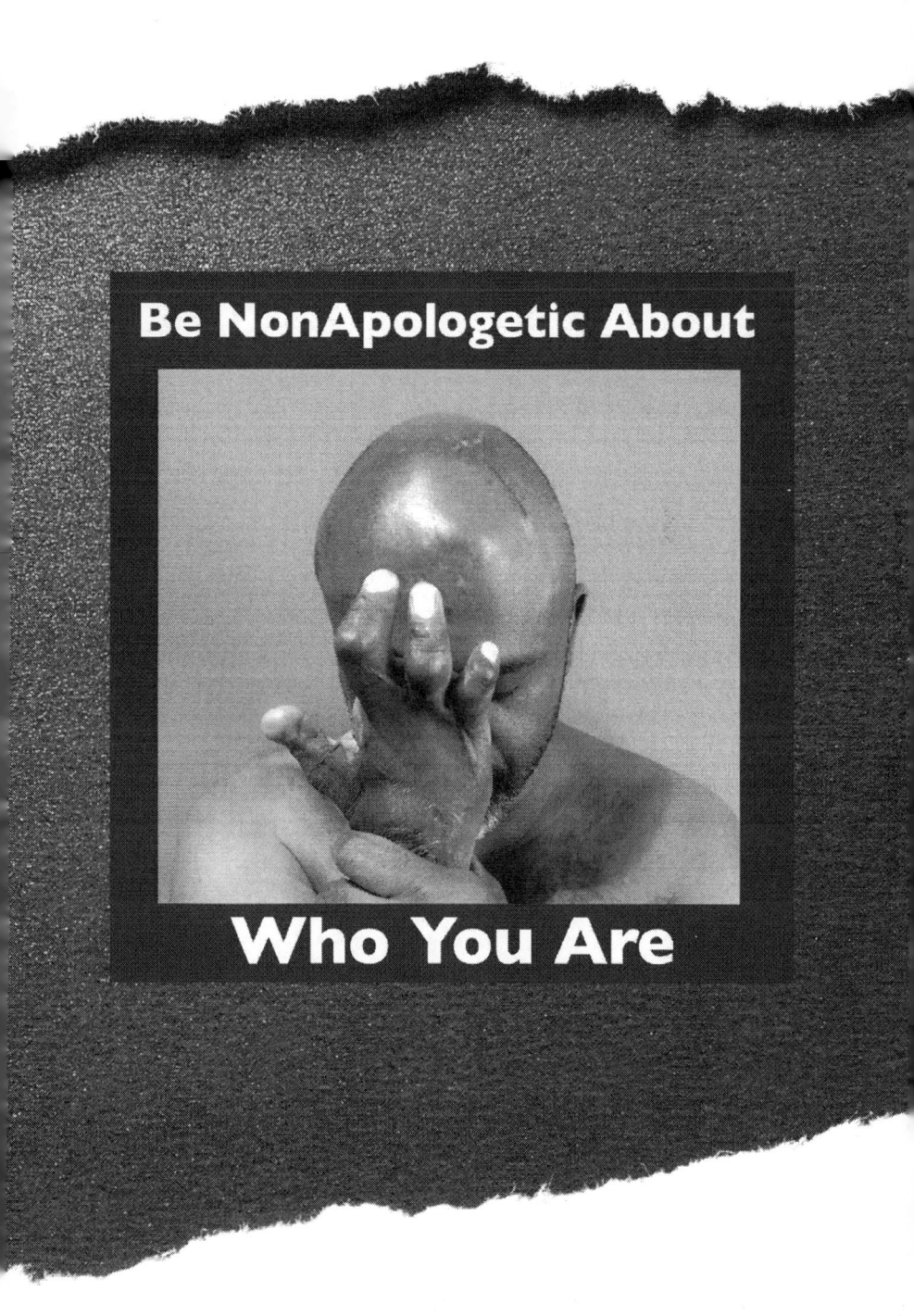

Show The World Who You Are

Tell Them

Who You Are

Be Bold About Who You Are

Laugh About Who You Are

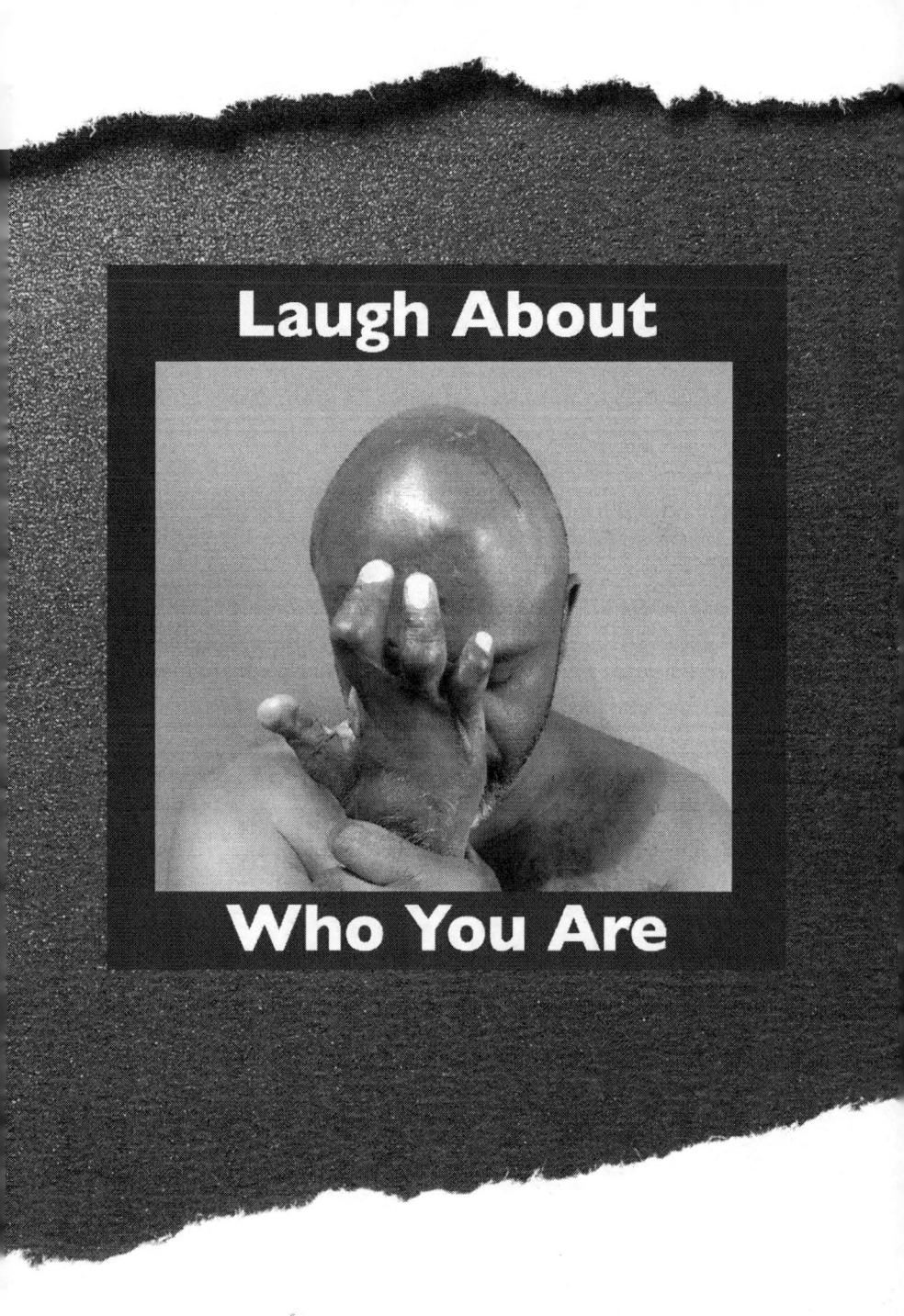

Respect

Who You Are

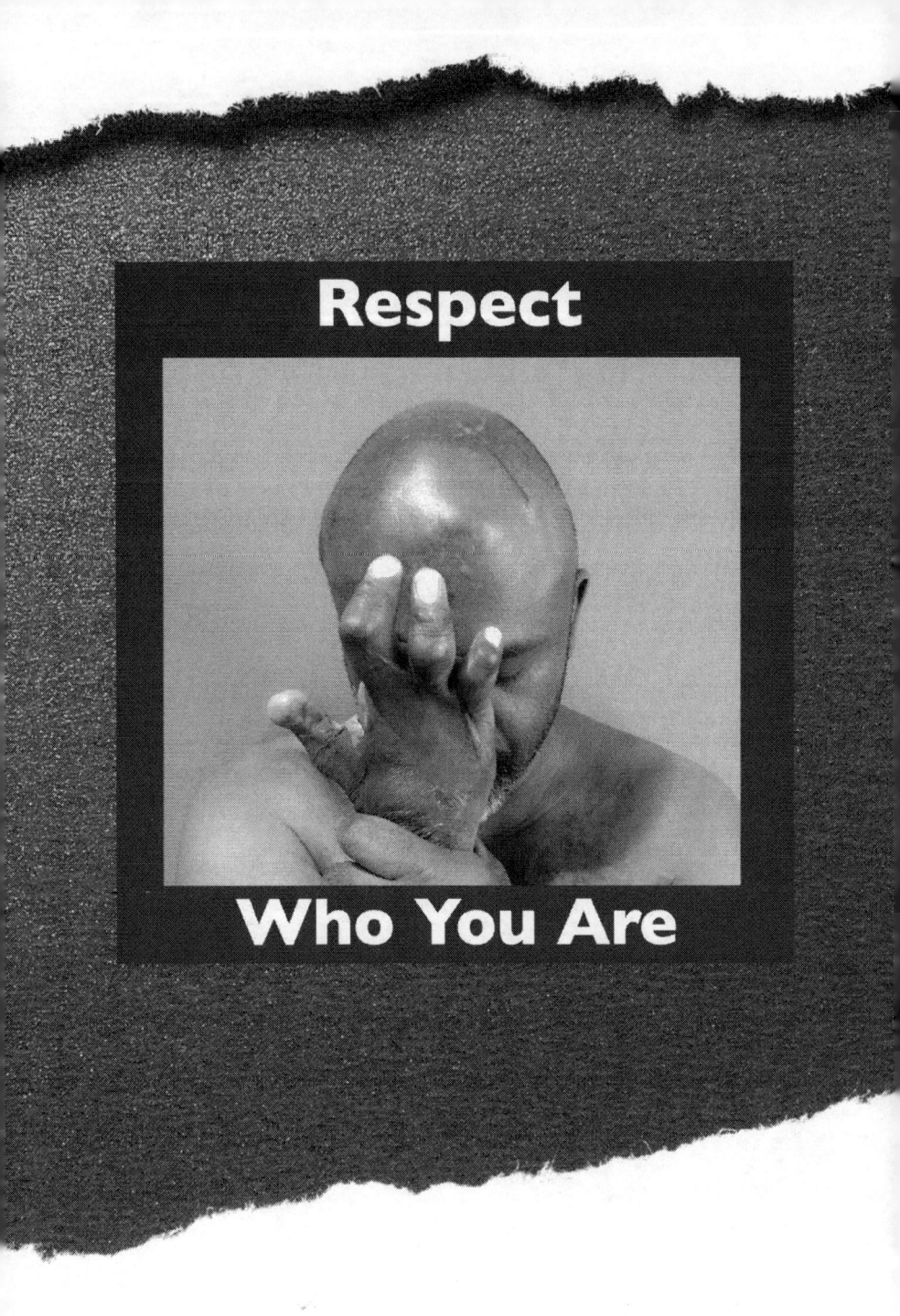

Like

Who You Are

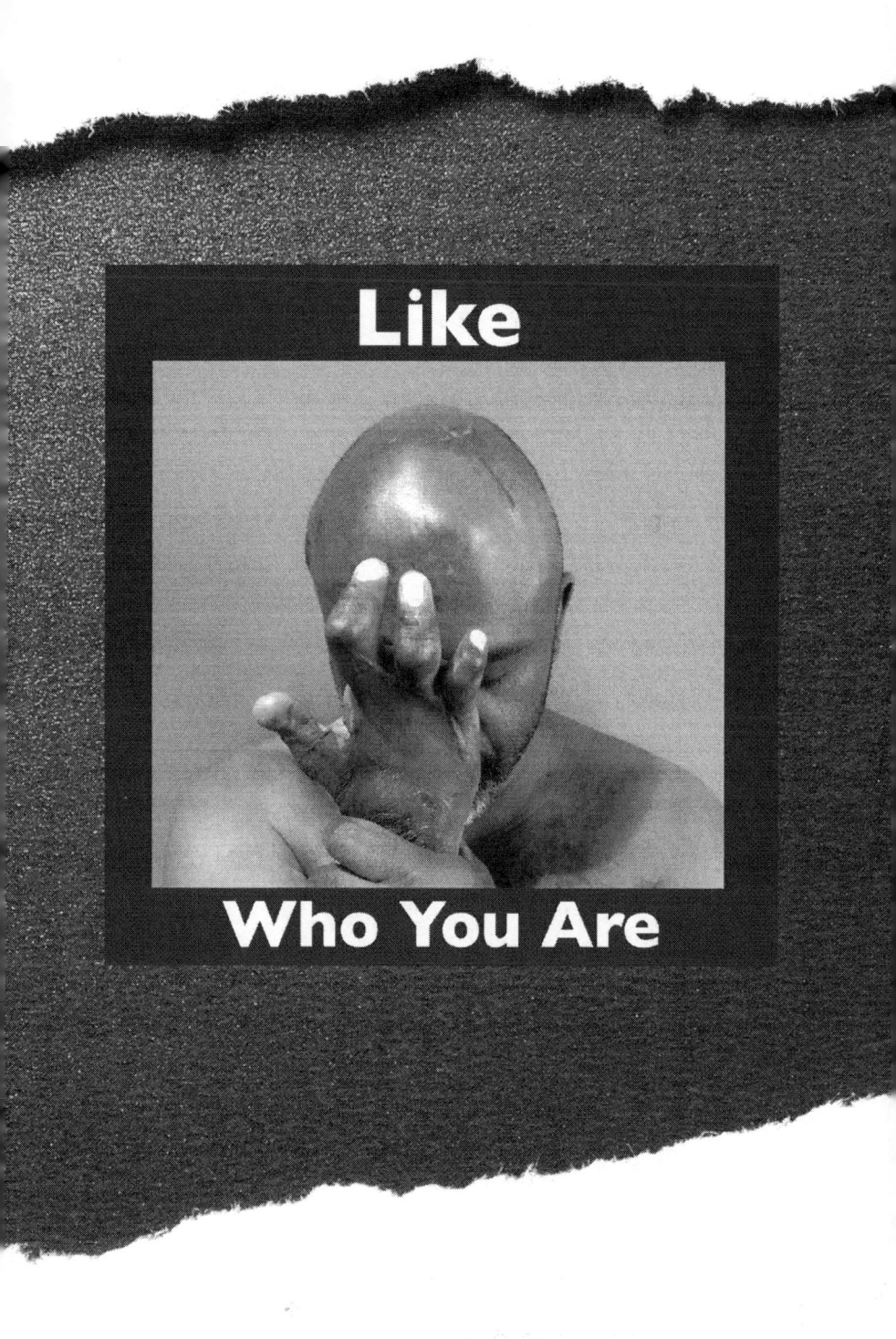

Love

Who You Are

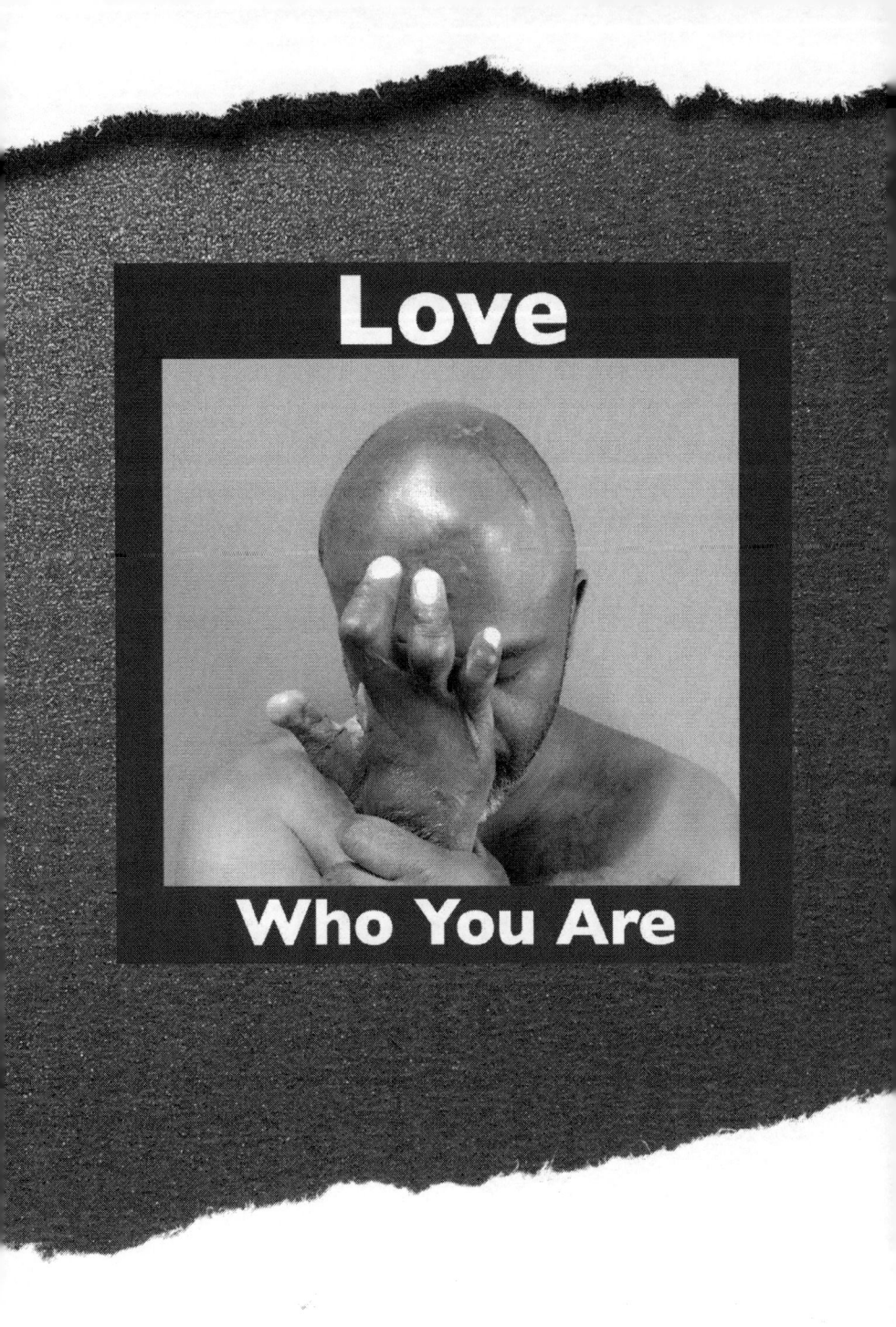

No One Needs to Approve Who You Are

Jesus Loves Who You Are

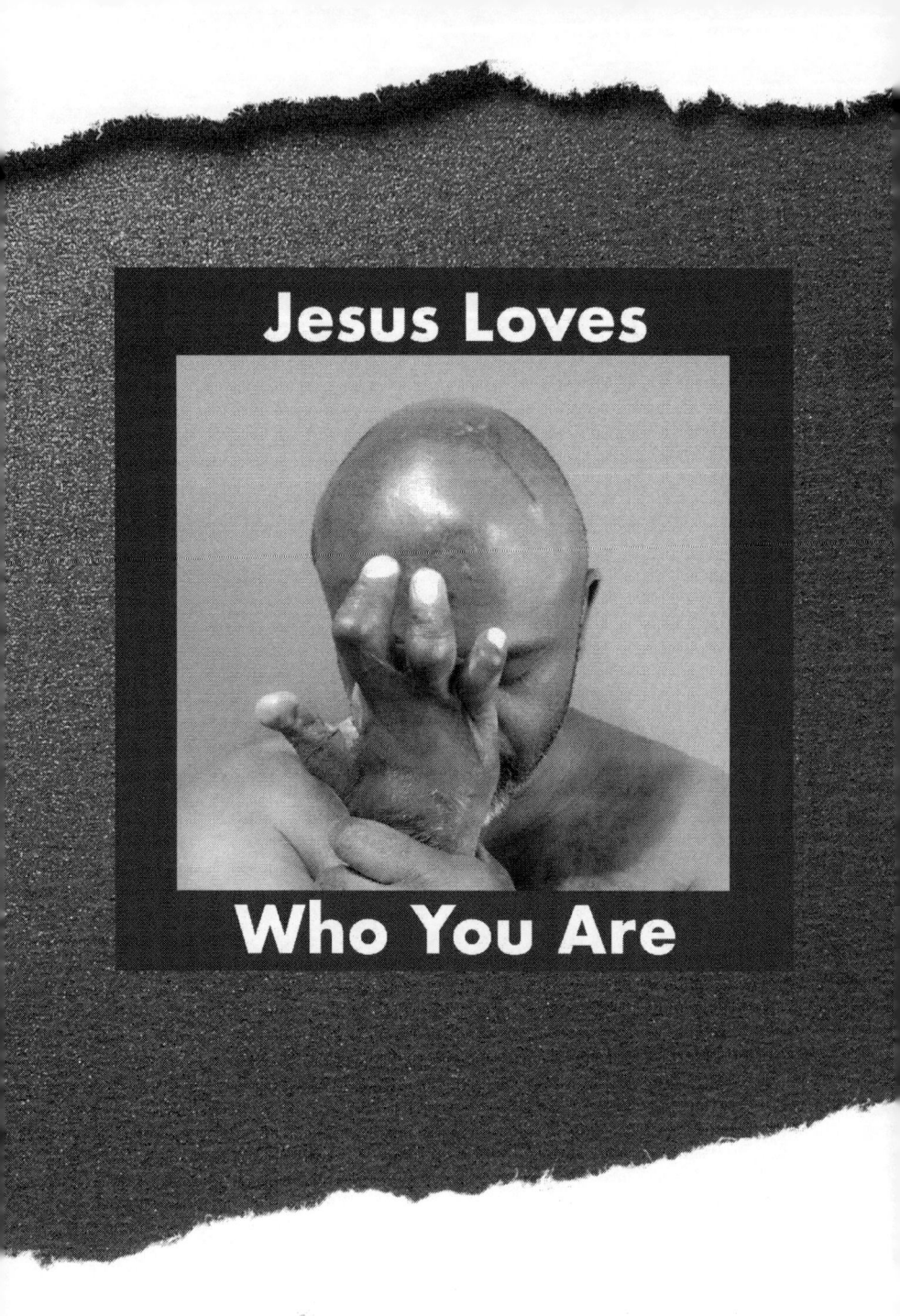

I'M REGGIE HATHORN

I dedicate this book to all the Lil Reggie's out there –

To every kid or person that felt different.
Every kid that cried by themselves.
Every kid that hid a part or all of themselves.
Every kid that felt like no one loved them.
Every kid that held in their tears.
Every kid that was picked on.
Every kid that wanted to be somebody else.
Every kid that felt misunderstood.
Every kid that felt like they didn't have anyone to talk to.
Every kid that felt left out.

I understand.
Love,
Reggie

A WORD FOR MY PARENTS

I'm gone make this simple. Y'all are the shit - period.

One thing I'm sure of is that y'all gave me your best and that's all I could ever ask for. Let's be real, y'all were just kids yourselves when you had me. Y'all were raising a black boy with a disability in the 70s and 80s, and y'all knocked that shit out the park. Y'all did the absolute best with what you had. You did what you knew how to do, and I love y'all for that.

Mama, you are the epitome of beauty, support, understanding and love. You already know you will forever be my main squeeze.

Pops you are my ambassador of cool, realness, and encouragement. You are my main Mufucka, but I think you know that. I am Coach Hathorn's son for life.

Thank y'all for everything - I mean everything. Thank y'all for teaching me everything y'all knew and for having the patience, courage and acceptance to watch me learn the shit y'all didn't know how to teach me.

I owe everything to y'all.

Thank y'all for giving me the best of yourselves. I love you, love you, love you.

You two are aight wit' me. Y'all did an amazing job.

Y'all are my MUFUCKAS for life!

Mama, I know you ain't a fan of the word Mufucka - but this here is MY book. Hahahaha

A MESSAGE TO THE READERS

Thanks for taking the time to read this portion of my journey. Trust me, there's so much more to share.

I also hope you gathered that Mufucka is not just a word for me - it's a way of life, it's a frame of mind, it's a state of being. It's liberating. It's me speaking at my highest volume. It's me at my highest level of authenticity. It's me saying I don't give a fuck because my true voice had been suppressed for too long. It's time to shout in my purest, most honest voice.

May you find that word or thing that puts you in the space that Mufucka puts me in.

Now that I've said that -

I know each of you got something different from reading this book. I hope it inspired you to either grow in some kinda way, heal in whatever way you need to heal, or accept that piece of yourself that will give you permission to live a fulfilling life.

I hope you can see that healing is ongoing and it happens in phases. And in some cases it doesn't happen at all. I hope that's not the case for you. But it seems like healing is never ending. I don't know yet. And everyone's journey is totally different. It took a lot of journaling and therapy for me. It may not take the same for you. But whatever it takes, I pray it happens for you.

Self-acceptance, for me, has been the same way, meaning it happens in phases and it's ongoing. I just showed you a glimpse of the shit that I went thru. Me pulling my hand out of my pocket was a major moment of self-acceptance. And I'm still not done. I couldn't force it. I'm still putting in work and being extremely intentional. But everyone is different. Everyone needs a different type of motivation. I pray you get the type of motivation you need to accept those things about you or your life that have been blocking you from living authentically and wholly.

I can only tell you my story and what has worked for me. You may have been looking for something new to try and maybe reading *Mufucka* has inspired you to try some of the shit that has worked for me. Or maybe it just confirms that you just might be on the right track. Hell, I don't know. But I hope you find that thing that works for you. I want that for you.

I pray for maximum growth, full healing, and total self-acceptance for all of you.

In a nutshell, thanks for going on this journey with me.

And please, please, please don't forget to evolve.

Y'all be careful out there in them streets - and I'm Reggie Hathorn.

ACKNOWLEDGEMENT

I want to give a special thanks to all my family, friends, colleagues, and random mufuckas who I've met along the way that have supported my journey throughout the years. You know who you are because I've thanked you personally. And plus I ain't bout to have someone say I missed their name - fuck that. You guys are fucking awesome. I could never repay you guys for what you've done for me, so a big ass thanks is going to have to do.

Thank you to the people who've followed and grown with my social media brand over the last five years. I've been through some changes and you've hung in there. I can only hope that I've given you the encouragement and support that you've given me.

I love and appreciate you all from the bottom up.

Reggie

ABOUT THE AUTHOR

"Don't forget to evolve..."

Reggie Hathorn was born in Louisville, MS, raised in Pine Bluff, AR and currently lives in Chicago, IL. A twist of fate during a visit to Dallas, when his car ran out of gas, was the catalyst for a huge change and that one lost weekend led to him staying and living in the city for 20 years.

Reggie attended both Jackson State and the University of Minnesota, receiving a dual degree in Mathematics and Electrical Engineering and has enjoyed an eclectic working life as a High School math teacher, sales manager and entrepreneur. He currently owns a candle store in Chicago, selling candles that promote mental health awareness and inspire self-acceptance, a business he started from a kitchen in a one room apartment.

With a love of writing he felt that this experience, as well as other childhood challenges, could help others. His book, **Muf*cka: A Bold New Perspective on Growth, Healing and Self-Acceptance**, looks back at the moments that came close to breaking him in his childhood, how he defeated them and others can beat them too. It is a fresh, honest and very different read from other self-help styled books on the subject.

In his free time Reggie enjoys taking long walks, eating ice cream in the park and people watching in hotel bars and lounges. He is also a fan of staycations, a good movie, cookies and old time singers, Frank Sinatra and Sammy Davis Jnr.
Always one who has wanted to give back wherever possible, Reggie regularly reads to the elderly residents of a senior assistant home in his neighborhood. His longstanding dream has been to travel the world and inspire others and he is already halfway towards reaching that goal.

You can contact or follow Reggie Hathorn at:
Facebook: Reggie Hathorn
Instagram: Reggie Hathorn
Website: www.imreggiehathorn.com